Into the Okavango

Into the Okavango

The Africa Poems and Photographs

Poems

by

Marianne Harding Burgoyne

Photographs

by

Marianne Harding Burgoyne

and

Robert H. Burgoyne, M.D.

Burgoyne and Burgoyne, Publishers

Paragon Press

Master Printers since 1924

Salt Lake City

First published in the United States
by Burgoyne and Burgoyne, Publishers, in 2005.
Produced by Burgoyne and Burgoyne, Publishers

Library of Congress Control Number: 2003099168
Marianne Harding Burgoyne
Into the Okavango: The Africa Poems and Photographs / Marianne Harding Burgoyne

Printed and bound in Salt Lake City
Distributed by Baker & Taylor, Inc., at www.btol.com and at
www.burgoyneandburgoynepublishers.com
First edition

ISBN 0-9742183-0-8

1. Photography—Salt Lake City, New York, Johannesburg, Maun, Savuti, Khwai, Moremi,
   Mowana, Chobe, Victoria Falls, Jijima, Hwange, Harare, Cutty Sark, Lake Kariba, Cape
   Town, Franschhoek, Stellenbosch, Cape Point. 2. Poetry. I. Burgoyne, Marianne Harding.
   II. Title.

Burgoyne and Burgoyne, Publishers
P.O. Box 17095
Salt Lake City, UT 84117-0095
Telephone: (801) 277-8977
Fax: (801) 277-7789
Toll-free Telephone: (877) 278-8977
Toll-free Fax: (877) 278-7789
E-mail: burgoyne@burgoyne.com
www.burgoyneandburgoynepublishers.com
Symposiums on the book
may be scheduled with the author.

Key to Photographers

- Marianne Harding Burgoyne
- Robert H. Burgoyne, M.D.
- Marie Antoinette (Toni) Burgoyne
- Rodney (Rod) W. Burgoyne, M.D.
- Grant Heaton
- Howie Garber
- Nancy Rich Knight
- Guides
- Others; specified with photo

Reference Key

- Marianne, on-site
- Guides, hosts, and/or bushmen
- Itinerary
- Maps
- Visitor's Center
- *National Audubon Society Field Guide to African Wildlife*
- *The Behavior Guide to African Mammals*
- *Okavango: Sea of Land, Land of Water*
- *Okavango: Africa's Last Eden*
- Encarta Encyclopedia
- *Patterns in the Grass.* (National Geographic video)

To Robert, my reassuring husband,
who has shown my family and me a better way—
Thanks and thanks again and ever thanks.

And to my cats—my family—
whose skillful antics and stellar hearts
have brought us joy.

In memory of
Tess of the Bourgognes
December 22, 1981–June 27, 1997

Isilwane of the Bourgognes
March 22, 1995–Present

In memory of
Xaxaba of the Bourgognes
March 7, 1998–April 23, 1999

Ihlosi of the Bourgognes
April 11, 1999–Present

If you can imagine it, you can achieve it.
If you can dream it, you can become it.

—William Arthur Ward

Contents

Half-title page:
🦁 *Feature:* Lion cub—Here's looking at you; Fothergill Island

Frontispiece:
🦁 *Feature:* Young majestic male lion; Savuti

Dedication page:
🐊 *Background:* Robert, Marianne, and Tess; photograph by Dave Newman

Epigraph photo:
🐘 *Background:* Tess of the Bourgognes

Cobra, lowermost right of recto pages:
🐍 Bronze cobra; Burgoyne art collection

Animal prints across lower recto and verso pages:
🐆 *National Audubon Society Field Guide to African Wildlife*

From America to Africa and into the Wild

I was born wanting to go to Africa. Why, it's hard to say—the call of the primal, an affinity with cats, the lure of undiscovered country, the danger, the forbidden, the face of death. The desire became a quest on a train bound, of all places, from Shanghai to Beijing in 1987. I sat with friends, urging them to make my desire theirs. No one was willing.

My husband and I scheduled a safari with his brother and wife, Rod and Toni Burgoyne, to Botswana, Zimbabwe, and South Africa in April 1997. Six weeks before our departure, our beloved cat was diagnosed with lymphoma. We canceled our trip—now my brother-in-law won't travel with us—and administered chemotherapy to our dear Tess. She died of kidney failure in June. She had been my only cat. We buried her in the backyard and rescheduled our "wings" trip in August.

There's only one flight a day from New York to Johannesburg, leaving at 6:20 p.m. on South African Airways. We managed to survive the fourteen-and-a-half-hour flight, checking into a typical Holiday Inn. The next morning, we stored our excess luggage in the Johannesburg Airport, taking only twenty-five pounds of baggage into Botswana, including camera equipment—a challenge, especially for this female.

We flew to Maun, cleared customs, separated ourselves from those tourists carrying guns, and met our first bush pilot—a twenty-three-year-old. If that thought wasn't scary, his thirty-year-old, single-engine Cessna was. I admit, I felt like Karen Blixen, flying low over Africa's vast wilderness. Below were nothing but baked brown earth, dried-up riverbeds, and bush fires blazing out of control, sending up smoke signals.

I saw only one animal from the air—an elephant, who seemed not so threatening compared to the Cessna. I still hear the roaring clamor of its engine, the rickety jiggle of the cockpit panel. Another Cessna outside the pilot's window, and suddenly we were in a drag race to the finish—a dirt runway near Savuti. We won. Phineas, our guide, was waiting in a four-wheel open Land Rover. Already, I felt exposed, breathless, anticipating three weeks of safaris ahead of us.

Our first camp was luxurious: twin beds with mosquito netting, custom-made sisal carpeting with hand-painted ethnic designs, double washbasins, a shower as big as a walk-in closet. The furniture had been built in Zimbabwe of local kiaat timber. We weren't exactly roughing it, not with hot water, hair dryers, and same-day laundry service, a necessity considering the few clothes we had. We learned later the camp was run by Orient Express Hotels. That night, we dined in our first open-air boma, the hosts serving a dinner fit for royalty.

Later, by the campfire, the Cimmerian night, without lights from any city nearby, touched the sand. I felt a chill. In this hemisphere, the sky turned on itself; Scorpius had overthrown Orion. We were told we could not walk back to our tent unaccompanied by a guide. "Hyenas," Phineas said, "come into camp this late," and I knew

> only few men go
> flaming, forbidden into
> the Okavango.

From America...

Photographs this page:

Upper right: Tess of the Bourgognes, 1990; Burgoyne bedroom

Middle right: Tess's grave, four days after her burial; Burgoyne backyard

Lower right: Tess, feral again, seven days before she died

Lower left: Tess of the Bourgognes, Christmas 1990; Burgoyne living room

Lower middle left: Tess on Turkish silk-on-silk carpet, among paperwhites

Upper middle left: Lilies bloom on Tess's death day: June 27, 1997

Upper left: Marianne and Tess, five days before Tess died

xi

To Africa...

International Arrivals / Ba Ba Tswang Go Sele

And into the Wild

Photographs opposite page:

🐾 *Upper right:* Robert and Marianne, traveling to Johannesburg; photograph by passenger

🐘 *Middle right:* Robert with first bush pilot; A2-CHE single-engine Cessna; Maun to Savuti

🐾 *Lower right:* Sign; Maun International Airport

🐘 *Lower left:* Marianne, scared; Johannesburg Holiday Inn

🐾 *Lower middle left:* Camera bag, containing Nikon 90

🐘 *Upper middle left:* South African Airways; New York

🐾 *Upper left:* Twenty-five pounds of baggage per person

Photographs this page:

🐘 *Upper right:* Land Rover; Savuti Airport

🦤 *Middle right:* Marianne and Robert; Savuti *boma*

🐘 *Lower right:* Double washbasins; Savuti hut

🐾 *Lower left:* Double beds with mosquito netting; Savuti hut

🦚 *Middle left:* Phineas, Franco Delle Piane, Marianne, and Robert; Savuti; photograph by Nina Delle Piane

🐘 *Upper left:* Phineas, Savuti guide

xiii

Acknowledgments

Into the Okavango: The Africa Poems and Photographs would never have become a reality without the sustaining, optimistic support of my husband, Robert. In 1999, after wr just a few poems and sending them with sample photographs, I queried eleven publishers, including Ohio University Press, Renaissance Books, and Sierra Club Books. Most ed responded personally with the same message: lovely, well organized—too expensive. One night in bed, I said to Robert, "This Africa project will go the way of the novel—into drawer." He said, "No, it won't. We will do it ourselves." From that moment forward, I envisioned the entire book. I even had nightmares that someday, once the book published, I would panic at the idea of "what if" I hadn't chosen to proceed because the book was taking on a life of its own. I credit my husband for investing in a young wo with dismal prospects, propping her on her feet, and enabling her to create a thing of beauty she birthed like a child.

This book has, nevertheless, been completed against tremendous odds. During the two-year process (2001–2003) of creating the book with Paragon Press, I lost fifteen people c to me, including my mother, my brother, my grandmother aunt, three other aunts, two cousins, and seven closest friends or extended family. My husband has survived pros cancer, the loss of his left eye, and a near-death experience with cellulitis and resulting renal failure. My nephew-in-law survived a near-fatal motorcycle accident with a contin difficult recovery, and now my young sister Jeanne, who never smoked, has been diagnosed with stage-four lung cancer. Through this march of death, I stopped often to care for family. I couldn't have done otherwise. To my critics who have asked, "Is this book ever coming out?" or "How many years has it been?" I answer, "My family comes first." I always been only a part-time writer. After endless stops, I finally brought this book to the marketplace.

Nor has the book been easy to finance. A small inheritance from my mother, Lurean Stevens Harding, along with a small bequest from my Aunt Nona Stevens Smith, finan nearly three-fourths of the book. My husband worked diligently to finance the rest, postponing retirement. His gift of taking me to Africa made his contribution nearly equal to m such that we are fifty-fifty partners in Burgoyne and Burgoyne, Publishers. We didn't necessarily risk our financial security, but we obliterated our cash flow for several ye Reflecting on this struggle, I remember the words of Marcel Proust: "We must never be afraid to go too far because success lies just beyond."

A few good men and women helped put this book together. I thank my contributing photographers: my husband, Robert; his brother and sister-in-law, Rod and Toni Burgoyne; G Heaton for photographing my icons; nature photographer Howie Garber; friend Nancy Rich Knight, who advised me to take the South Africa "wings" trip; family photographer D Newman; and nature photographer Joe McDonald.

Spiro and Maria Nichols of Nichols Photo Lab Inc. developed and reprinted my negatives. Mr. Nichols offered advice throughout the project, and Geri Mills, color anal reprinted photographs to exacting specifications. Two receptionists, Sarah Beyers and Michelle Earle, transacted my business with care and steady concern.

I thank the guides in Africa who expanded our knowledge of Africa's animals: Phineas, Deluxe, Killer, Sam, Dean, and John, who are written up in the poems. I also thank gui Guy Dudley of Gametrackers in Botswana for e-mails after the trip, helping me identify birds and mammals, and Malcolm Robinson, operations manager, also of Gametrackers. his 2:00 a.m. return telephone call, confirming the names of other birds and mammals. (I awakened him when I first contacted him.) He asked, "What time is it there?" teasing for my absent-minded 1:00 a.m. call to him.

I thank the exuberant team at the marvelous Utah's Hogle Zoo: Kimberly Davidson, assistant director; Jane Larson, animal care supervisor; and Rich Hendron, education curator, reviewing my blueline and helping me fine-tune label the animals according to race, not simply species. Brown Floral, Every Blooming Thing, Western Garden Center (Con Thompson), and Ensign Wholesale helped identify flowers when efforts to contact Kirstenbosch Botanical Gardens never materialized, nor did searches on Amazon.com to f *Flowers of Southern Africa* result in success. I left two flowers unidentified. I claim only amateur status in creating this book.

I thank Paragon Press for a dedicated two-year effort: Al Fairbanks, president, who oversaw financial concerns; Steven Larson for preliminary suggestions of the layout design; D Leiker and John Churchill, scanner operators, for their design work and color corrections I approved. I thank Nadia Fenton for her computer assembly; her analytical questioni moving the project to error-free status; and especially for her work adding the difficult key to 216 pages, no easy task. Receptionist Jodi Griffiths transferred a thousand calls to Mi Perkins, project director. *Into the Okavango* never could have been completed without Mike's untiring dedication. Extraordinary, Mike is a "Yes, we can do this" man who ma things happen that otherwise wouldn't have. For example, he made the French Script font work when I had been told it couldn't; he replaced photographs with reprints when wasn't satisfied with the original quality and pressed to get small Africa animals for the keys. The list goes on. I laid out every page; Mike oversaw the fulfillment of all instruction I told Al that the smartest move he ever made was to choose Mike Perkins to head my project. I told Mike I wouldn't hesitate to make him project director of my next book; we work so congenially together. His talent and patience facilitated our work. A former student, George Furgis, endorsed Paragon Press.

Regarding the poems, I thank two very special women. Lisa Bickmore, an established Utah poet, much more experienced than I, agreed to read my poems and offer objecti criticism. We met every two weeks for a school year (1999–2000) to revise the poems. She read the first draft of poems, pulling those she wouldn't touch, and saying of the re "You can't leave yourself out of the poems." Coming off a failed autobiographical novel, I had written simple poems about the animals—they eat, drink, sleep, mate, and kill—wi little mention of myself. She encouraged me not to be afraid to tell the dark, parallel story that now accompanies the simplicity of the animal poems. The result is that the book te two stories. One is of the twenty-three days of safaris through South Africa, Botswana, and Zimbabwe. As the safaris get more dangerous, the camps more remote, the poet embar on a darker journey to the sad, painful places of her soul, not often visited. The poems, then, have become a shadow of my unpublished novel. I thank Lisa for her kindness, h encouragement, and her genuine willingness to help without snobbish superiority. She has helped me more professionally than anyone else I know.

The second woman I thank is Barbara Bannon, my copy editor. Our relationship goes back to when we both wrote for *Utah Holiday*. She was my copy editor then, too. Barbara ha a great eye for catching my hyphen, one-word-or-two errors. She also standardized the plurals of my animals against one source: *Merriam-Webster's Collegiate Dictionary, Ten Edition.* Barbara acted as my security blanket, saying, "I am here to hold your hand" when we read the signature copies and signed off on them together. Barbara is a brillia wonderful person who is underpaid for her talented knowledge of the English language.

I thank Kedar Rugg at Burgoyne Computers for setting up my Web page, as well as the entire staff for keeping my computer—my pen—working, and Kelly Dumont, comput specialist at Jordan School District, for teaching me to do "hot keys," making completion of the book's keys faster. I thank my secondary sources, which are acknowledged in th footnote key and bibliography.

I thank a very special father and mother in the Midwest for allowing me to photograph their beautiful daughter, Missy, her brothers, and cousins at play. What a great family they ar I still can't get over how the father knew where Missy's last year's swimming suit was or how much mother and daughter look alike. Our friendship continues—a blessing.

I thank those few friends, especially one, who never gave up on the project, encouraging me to the end.

Perhaps the biggest risk I have taken with this book is placing photographs of my four beloved cats alongside the African cats. I couldn't resist; they are so much a part of me "The smallest feline is a masterpiece," said Leonardo da Vinci. My four have been my children. I can't sign off without thanking God for making them and all creature bright and beautiful.

Marianne Harding Burgoyne
September 25, 2003

Postscript: My sister Jeanne died untimely the same hour I finished writing these acknowledgments, one month after she was diagnosed, slipping away on the infusion table momen before her first chemotherapy injection. Her husband, Stott, was at her side. She leaves him, two daughters, one son, two sons-in-law, and six grandchildren.

Into the Okavango,

Where few men go,
the Okavango
and other rivers
search in vain for the sea.
Waters from Angola highlands,
labyrinthine pathways,
dense with papyrus,
meander impotently,
unable to escape the destiny
of the Kalahari sand.

Monsoon rains
flood the vast inland delta,
then shrink when the charring sun
scorches water into salt pans.
Wildlife thrives.
Hippopotamuses and crocodiles
patrol the rivers;
kudu, waterbuck,
lechwe, impala roam,
and the great zebra migration

tracks
single
file

across the parched, cracked land.
Lions mate and kill,
cheetah cubs play like kittens,
the covert leopard
leaves the remains
of a warthog
on a baobab limb.
Poachers annihilate
the rhinoceroses,
shoot elephants for tusks.

In this sanctuary for birds,
the African fish eagle
hunts mornings for tiger fish;
bushmen pole dugout canoes
through watery highways
searching for food.
Women gather plants
for perfume
and water-lily bulbs
for evening stew.

Strange,
when this sanctuary
holds such treasures,
the world is not rushing
to preserve its beauty.
For two million years,
the rivers searing and
roaring with life-giving force
now are threatened
by a final vanishing act:

farmers draining the delta
for agriculture,
an unrepentant blunder—
unrequited mirage
of unimaginable loss.
Some corners of the world
must remain untouched.

Into the Okavango,
let few men go. . . .

Savutí

The elephants stand like monuments at the watering hole.

Savuti

The elephants stand
like monuments
at the watering hole.
Less water, more mud,
yet they drink
and bathe, content;
the watering holes
never quite give out.
Later, in a circle,
as if performing
some ancient ritual,
the mammals shade themselves
under a single acacia tree.
This is Savuti,
the elephant camp,
where elephants trumpet
half the night
just outside our tent;
hyenas laugh,
tearing at their prey.
I dream of Stonehenge
and then lie awake wondering
how many impala
will die before morning
on the savanna.

Savutí

Page 1:
🐘 *Feature:* Botswana from the air

Page 2:
🐘 *Feature:* Baked brown earth and dried up riverbeds; Botswana

Camp title page:
🐘 *Feature:* African elephant, eating; Savuti

Premier camp photograph:
🐘 *Feature:* African elephants outside camp; Savuti

Photographs opposite page:
🐘 *Upper right:* Entrance to Savuti sign

🐘 *Middle right:* African elephants, bathing; Savuti watering hole

🐘 *Lower left:* Verdite elephant; Burgoyne art collection

🐘 *Middle center:* Bronze elephant, front; Burgoyne art collection

🐘 *Upper center:* Bronze elephant, back; Burgoyne art collection

Photograph this page:
🐘 *Feature:* African elephant herd under acacia camel thorn tree; Savuti

7

I dream of Stonehenge...

Savutí

Photographs opposite page:

Upper right: Stonehenge, September 1981

Middle right: African elephants, bathing; Savuti watering hole

Lower left: African elephant, walking across savanna; Savuti

Middle left: Wooden African elephant; Burgoyne art collection

Photographs this page:

Feature: Impala, seeking refuge under trees; Chobe

Lower left: Spotted hyenas, greeting each other; Savuti

Morning Kill

Three cheetahs sit stoic
on the mound waiting.
They seem not to breathe.
So still, they wait.
They do not track but stalk.
Hidden in marsh grass,
they ambush antelope
for their morning meal.

They sit picture perfect
with tear-stained,
clown-painted faces,
hungry and intent,
but selective. A kudu
ambles by unhindered,
protected by a baobab,
unaware.

A herd of impala
wanders near.
So stealthy the cats,
the impala show no fear.
They graze, the rising sun
glossing their tawny coats.
Sandgrouse chatter overhead,
Oh No, gonna do it aGain.
Oh No, gonna do it aGain.

Savutí

Photographs opposite page:

 *Upper right:* Baobab tree; Savuti

Middle right: Mother and cheetah cubs, listening; Savuti

Middle center: Female greater kudu, alert; Savuti

Photograph this page:

Feature: Mother and cheetah cubs, wary; Savuti

11

It happens at once.
The cats spring; one impala falls.
The others bound terrified
across the marsh.
The kill disappears from view
in wheat too tall to see.
The kudu vanishes.
Sandgrouse scatter:
Oh No, gone and done it aGain.
No Gain, No Gain.

I do not witness the feast,
except to say
the grass turns red.

Savutí

Photographs opposite page:

Upper right: Impala, greater kudu, and sandgrouse; Pump Pan

Middle right: Cheetah and cub, hunting; Savuti

Middle left: Wooden cheetah head; hand carved in Kenya

Uppermost left: Sandgrouse; Pump Pan

Photographs this page:

Feature: Cheetahs, eating after kill; Savuti

Lower left: Cheetah in grass; Savuti

13

Most Beautiful Cat

I saw the cheetah
standing
swaybacked
near the termite mound.
Alert,
poised,
questioning
her whereabouts,
she was lithesome,
sexy,
the siren
of the savanna.

Through my lens
I studied her:
large chest,
O'Hara waist,
provocative haunches;
I coveted
her delicate legs,
her cleatlike claws,
the perfect shape
of her elegant face.

Then she was off,
chasing a herd
of gazelles.
The bow of her body
sprang back,
then surged
like a greyhound,
airborne,
built to run.

Fetching female,
she swatted the hind leg
of a gazelle,
tripping it,
bringing it down;
clamped her jaws
around its neck.

Her kill was for her cubs,
but then she backed away,
outmanned by
a pack of hyenas
nearby.
Circling vultures
forced her to surrender.

Alone, defenseless—
this standoff
made me sad
no male
near
to protect her
or her young.

Savutí

Photographs opposite page:

Upper center: Cheetah cub, hissing; Savuti

Upper right: Termite mound; Savuti

Middle right: Alert cheetahs; Savuti

Upper left: Cheetah cubs, companions; Savuti

Photograph this page:

Feature: Most beautiful cheetah; Savuti

Identical Owls

Our guide Phineas,
as it turned out,
didn't miss a thing.
He jerked to a stop.
"What?" I asked.
He pointed to a tree.
Two white-faced owls
perched identically—
and, it seemed,
a bit angrily—
as I snapped my shutter.
They looked straight at me,
sending a double message.
What? I had no idea.
Did I disturb their sleep?
Were they after the rodent
beneath their lofty branch?

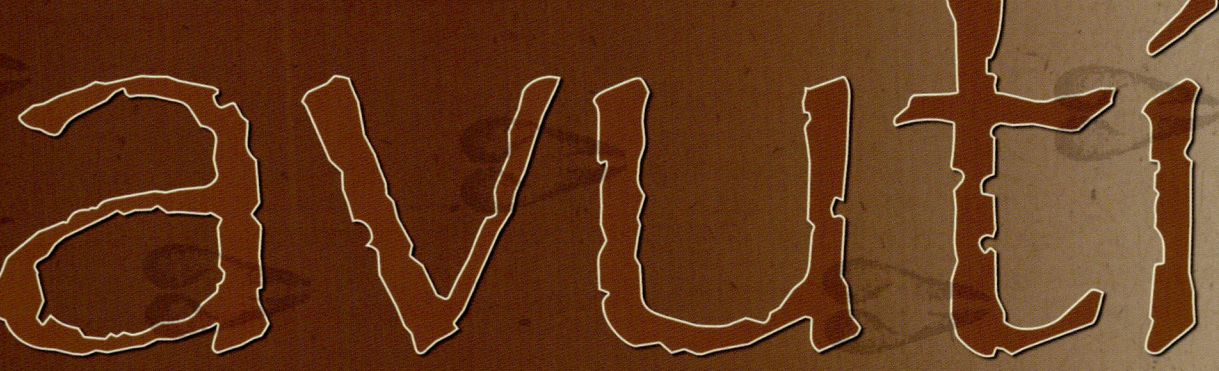

Savutí

Small Bundle of Shivers

During the afternoon
of our second day,
a solitary steenbok
crossed our path.
We stopped our Land Rover
for him.
His tiny legs sank
in the rich, red sand.
I thought he might disappear.
He seemed magical,
from another world,
this smallest antelope.

Once on the other side
of the road,
he stood still
by the trunk of a tree
and watched us
with ebony eyes,
ears back,
hair on end,
afraid to move.
I fancied he
must be hoping
we would travel on.

That night, I dreamed
this steenbok licked my face,
waking me.
"You're so cute,"
I exclaimed.
"What's your name?"
"Pip."
"I know Pip.
He lives on the moor."
"I live in your memory,"
he said without moving his lips
and bounded out of sight
before I could pet
the top of his head.

Photographs opposite page:

Feature: White-faced owls, gazing; Savuti

Lower left: Stylized hornbill spoons; Burgoyne art collection

Middle center: Tigereye necklace; Burgoyne jewelry collection

Photographs this page:

Upper right: Female steenbok, crossing road; Savuti

Middle right: Male steenbok, seeking refuge by tree trunk; Chobe

17

Like My Playful House Cats

I watched two cheetah cubs playing in a tree. The one who climbed higher had the advantage. She boxed at the other with her unsheathed claws, keeping him from jumping to meet her. Only when he gave up and ignored her, did she jump down and swat his hind legs to trip him, then wrestled him to the ground, climbed on top, conqueror for a day.

She scurried away, stood on her hind legs and stretched from a limb, then pounced again at her brother. They reminded me of my house cats having a good day, the baby not afraid to attack my big male, who, in turn, bites her by the neck to teach her his limits.

Savuti

Photographs opposite page:

Upper center: Cheetah, scratching tree; Savuti

Upper right: Cheetah, climbing tree; Savuti

Middle right: Cheetah, descending on sibling; Savuti

Lower center: Cheetah, beginning climb; Savuti

Middle center: African spear; Burgoyne art collection

Photographs this page:

Feature: Cheetah cub, playing in tree; Savuti

Lower left: Cheetah cub with an eye on sibling; Savuti

19

But cheetah cubs make
fetching meals
for lions and leopards.
These two could have been
from a litter of five.
Their mother must move
them every other day,
hoping they will be
overlooked.
Their mother called,
Ihn, Ihn,
high pitched
and persistent,
until the two cubs
broke off their play
and followed
her black-and-white
concentric and
conspicuous tail
into the thicket.

Savutí

Photographs opposite page:

Upper right: Xaxaba; ready to pounce on Isilwane; Burgoyne backyard

Middle right: Cheetah cubs and mother's concentric tail; Savuti

Lower left: Xaxaba by Tess's grave; Burgoyne backyard

Lower center: Isilwane, disciplining Xaxaba; Burgoyne backyard

Middle center: Isilwane, hidden in grass; Burgoyne backyard

Photograph this page:

Feature: Cheetah cub, dangling from a limb; Savuti

Roof Rescue

It could be anything—
wild as a stalking leopard
or harmless
as the veterinarian
wondering
if my Xaxaba's heart
had been too small
for anesthesia.
Accident or design:

All day,
I kept asking God—
as if he would—
to save the baby cubs.

Savutí

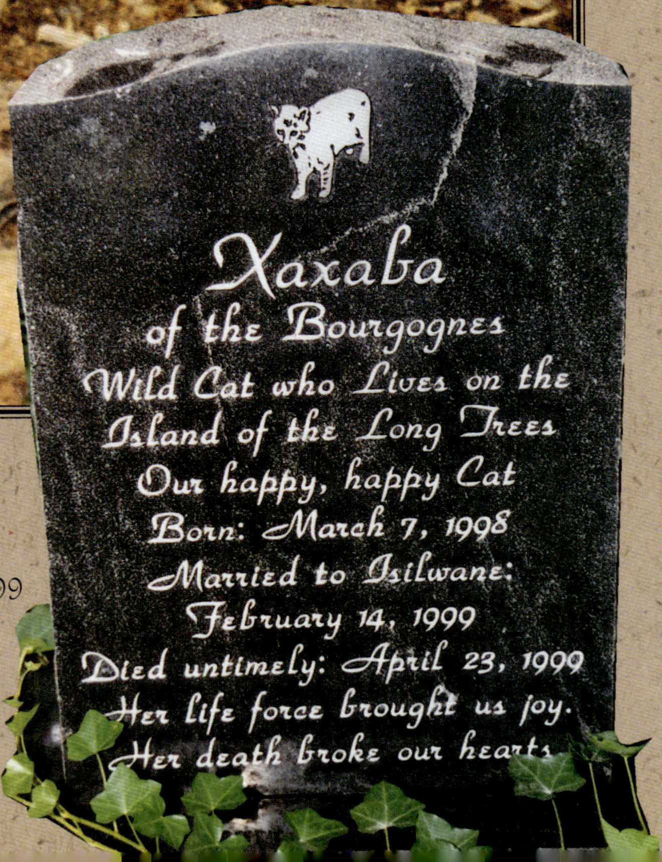

Xaxaba of the Bourgognes
Born: March 7, 1998
Died untimely: April 23, 1999

Photographs opposite page:

Upper right: Xaxaba on roof, pining for rescue; Burgoyne driveway

Middle right: Xaxaba, loving Isilwane in birdfeeder; Burgoyne backyard

Lower left: Mother cheetah; Savuti

Middle center: Cheetah cubs on lookout; Savuti

Upper center: Marianne, rescuing Xaxaba; Burgoyne driveway

Uppermost center: Marianne, grabbing Xaxaba from roof; Burgoyne driveway

Photographs this page:

Feature: Xaxaba, spring 1998; Burgoyne backyard

Lower right: Xaxaba's tombstone, summer 1999; Burgoyne backyard

Xaxaba
of the Bourgognes
Wild Cat who Lives on the
Island of the Long Trees
Our happy, happy Cat
Born: March 7, 1998
Married to Isilwane:
February 14, 1999
Died untimely: April 23, 1999
Her life force brought us joy.
Her death broke our hearts.

23

Distress Calls

I hear the red-billed hornbill
calling, wok, wok, wok.
He repeats himself rapidly,
wok-wok, wok-wok,
sounding an alarm.
Just now,
Savuti seems calm.
Looking around,
although I spy
a wild Eden,
nothing seems wrong.
This guy looks like
his own caricature.
Sooty with a white belly,
beady eyes,
and narrow red bill,
he mates for life
and uses the same nest
year after year.
Perhaps his mate is sealed
in a tree cavity
for twenty-four days,
hatching her eggs
and then waiting
for him
to bring food
to her young.
Wok-wok, wok-wok,
he keeps calling
without explaining
why he is complaining.

Savutí

Mating Rituals

I've read where the mating rituals of spotted hyenas include a bowing display, much like that of Anna and the King of Siam, only the other way around. The male, even the alpha male, must bow to the female. Once he does, one glare from her can send him scattering, plotting, for a week or two. She will eventually come around, especially if a group of males gangs up on her. Still, there must be bowing; males of successively higher rank come calling until she allows the alpha male, nose-to-tail, to mount. She's simply fussy; that's all.

Photographs opposite page:

Upper right: Red-billed hornbill, perched; Savuti

Middle right: Red-billed hornbill, enlarged; Savuti

Middle center: Amethysts; large stone from China; Burgoyne jewelry collection

Photographs this page:

Upper right: Spotted hyenas, female sending male scattering; Savuti

Middle right: Spotted hyenas, males bowing to female; Savuti

Lower left: Spotted hyenas, sitting along road; Savuti

25

On Seeing Lions for the First Time

Phineas stopped
the Land Rover abruptly.
He hopped out, stooped,
and drew a circle around the prints.
"Lions."
Determined we should see cats
our final day in Savuti,
he drove into the bush.
I heard my heart beat in my head.

Within ten minutes, he had tracked them:
two males, brothers likely,
a coalition defending turf.
They languished
in the midmorning sun,
aloof, bored with us.
We timidly snapped shutters
until the larger one got up
and walked directly toward the vehicle.

Phineas caught our eye
in the rearview mirror and whispered,
"Don't stand, don't talk, don't move,
don't do anything at all,
and he will walk around us."
I didn't breathe or take a picture
until the cat had cornered the van.
He hid himself behind a tree,
escaping publicity.

Savuti

Photographs opposite page:

Upper right: Two young male lions, brothers likely; Savuti

Middle right: Young male lion, resting; Savuti

Lower right: Lion prints on dirt road; Savuti

Photograph this page:

Feature: Young male lion, ignoring Land Rover; Savuti

Just when I thought I was safe,
stopped to reload my camera,
the other, who had been sleeping,
followed, moving so close
I could have touched him.
It wasn't until night
in our primitive tent,
spiders the size of half-dollars
on the wall,

I assessed
emotions
I had spent.
Too near their raw
and awful beauty,
overwhelmed by this peril,
this Eden,
I lay listening
to my husband's heart
and cried.

Savutí

Photographs opposite page:

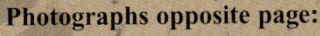 *Upper right:* Young male lion, sleeping; Savuti

Middle right: Young male lion, waking; Savuti

Lower left: Lion prints on dirt road, circled by Phineas; Savuti

Photographs this page:

Feature: Young male lion, escaping publicity; Savuti

Lower right: Young male lion, following brother; Savuti

Lower left: Spider, the size of a half-dollar; Cutty Sark

29

Sunset at Savuti

Sunset at Savuti
brings hyenas and elephants
to the same watering hole.
The hyenas seem brave,
although they sidestep
respectfully
when their rivals
want to drink.
A black-backed jackal circles nearby;
a lone eagle perches
on a background branch.
The land,
this moment,
cast the color
of a burning bush,
signals the fury
of coming night—
awful beauty at dusk,
silence before slaughter,
before the match strikes.

Savutí

Photographs opposite page:

Upper right: Black-breasted snake eagle on acacia camel thorn tree; Savuti

Middle right: Spotted hyenas, sidestepping African elephant; Savuti

Lower left: Black-backed jackal, circling; Savuti

Photograph this page:

Feature: African elephants, spotted hyenas, and black-breasted snake eagle at sunset; Savuti

Photograph next page:

Feature: Sunset; Savuti

Savutí

Khwai

On the banks of the Khwai, the hippopotamuses and crocodiles hang out together.

Hanging Out Together

On the banks of the Khwai,
   the hippopotamuses
and crocodiles
hang out together.
Not that they are friends;
they eat different things.
The hippos are barely visible.
I see their ears
and protruding eyes
and a hint of purple bulk,
their massive weight sinking
into mud beneath them.
I can't imagine they can float.

Four handsome creatures
are patterned so precisely
they are almost funny,
if they weren't so dangerous.
Herbivorous, they won't eat you,
although our guide Deluxe tells me,
"If they find you
in their water,
you will thrash
and drown,
even so."

Khwai

![Four common hippopotamuses resting in water with grassy riverbank behind]

Photographs opposite page:

Upper right: A2-ZFF single-engine aircraft; Savuti to Khwai

Middle right: Common hippopotamuses, resting along riverbank; Khwai

Lower center: Hut—sleeping quarters; spiders inside; Khwai

Camp title page:

Feature: Common hippopotamus, resting; Khwai

Premier camp photograph:

Feature: Common hippopotamuses and Nile crocodile, peaceful; Khwai

Photograph this page:

Feature: Four common hippopotamuses, patterned precisely; Khwai

But the Nile crocodile
slithers half submerged
along the bank,
his long snout camouflaged as
a floating log.
At once,
propelled by his tail,
he becomes a torpedo
of flashing teeth,
ambushing antelope
drinking at sunset
along the river.

The Nile crocodile
would rather have you for dinner.

Khwai

Photographs opposite page:

 Upper right: Marianne, Robert, and Deluxe on break; Khwai; photograph by accompanying guide

Middle right: Impala and young, drinking at sunset; Savuti

Lower left: Impala and young, observing photographer at sunset; Savuti

Photograph this page:

Feature: Nile crocodile, looking for dinner; Khwai

39

Still Life

From the River Khwai,
the impala moved slowly
in front of the Land Rover.
They stole by us in single file,
two-toned, saddle and tan glossy,
with slender, black-eyed, frightened faces,
moving deep into the golden grass,
traveling in a herd to protect their young.
They stopped cautiously and listened,
then turned in unison to face me—
the picture I had dreamed of—
before bounding across
the yellow savanna.

Khwai

Photographs opposite page:

Upper right: Impala, strolling in front of Land Rover; Khwai

Middle right: Impala, stopping to listen; Khwai

Middle left: Impala and young, cautious; Khwai

Photograph this page:

Feature: Impala and young, turning in unison; Khwai

41

Khwai

Lovesick

It's amazing the feats
males perform
for their females.
I saw the wattled crane
jumping high in an open field,
tossing grass into the air,
before I noticed his audience—
another splendid-looking crane
with her long white neck
extending her head and bill upward.

Again, he jumped high
and then dipped low,
bowing, asking for a dance.
He coiled his neck
over his back
and belted a shrill call.
She pierced back
the same high pitch,
assuming the same position.
They looked as if they were
breaking their necks
instead of enjoying each other.

I didn't see them mate,
these two with their gray wings
and black bellies,
red faces and little black caps.
But their courtship was splendid—
acrobatics, contortions,
figures of grace
prancing toward each other
in open wetlands.

Photograph opposite page:

Feature: Impala, bounding across savanna; Khwai

Photographs this page:

Upper right: Wattled crane, spying female; red lechwe in background; Khwai

Middle right: Wattled crane, object of desire; Khwai

Lower center: Bronze cranes; Andrea by Sadek; made in China; Burgoyne art collection

43

One's Own

The zebras were grazing
   in an open field,
watchful of their young
close by—
gentle as the ponies
in my neighbor's yard.
If I had been lucky enough
to witness a birth,
I would have seen the mare
lay claim.
When a foal is born,
its mother keeps it from seeing
any stripes but her own,
keeping the stallion and siblings,
the entire herd at bay,
twisting and turning around her young,
imprinting her pattern into
its awakening consciousness.
No zebra stripes are alike.
The foal must recognize its mother
by her myriad individual bands;
no other mother will claim it.

Khwai

Photographs opposite page:

 *Upper right:* Plains zebra, Chapman's race, with young; Khwai

Middle right: Plains zebra herd, Chapman's race, grazing, and wildebeest, eastern white-bearded race; Khwai

Lower left: Young plains zebra, Chapman's race, with visitors; Khwai

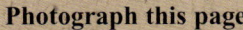

Photograph this page:

Feature: Plains zebra, Chapman's race, grazing; Khwai

45

Migrating ponies
search single file for grass
in the dry season.

Khwai

*S*tallions, seizing harems,
  rape pregnant mares;
      abduct prime fillies in heat.

Photographs opposite page:

Upper right: Plains zebras, Chapman's race, grazing; Khwai

Middle right: Plains zebras, Chapman's race, at dusk; Khwai

Middle left: Wooden zebra head; hand carved in Kenya

Upper middle left: Plains zebras, Chapman's race, migrating; Khwai

Photograph this page:

Feature: Plains zebras, Chapman's race, in alignment; Khwai

Brainy Beasts

Daylight is a good time for wildebeests.
They graze peacefully with zebras
in this northern boundary
of the Moremi Reserve.

Although they are antelope,
they seem more like cows
with their short, turned-up horns
and loose lips good for grazing.

At night, these animals rest in
linear bedding formations,
leaving enough space between them
to escape, should hyenas come hunting.

If they chose to lie in a circle,
those in the center would be trapped.
Smart-thinking antelope. I wonder if
their black beards have made them this wise.

Saddled

Colorful storks—
black heads and necks,
red bills with yellow saddles,
long, pencil legs,
red knobby knees,
and red unwebbed feet—
walk at the river's edge,
searching for fish.

Saddle-billed storks
eat anything:
frogs' legs,
locusts and lizards,
mollusks and lungfish.
They prefer to mate
and make babies;
count on storks to deliver.

He eyes her
with his black eye.
She stares back from yellow glass.
He runs ahead, then arrests her
with enormous, outspread wings,
looking like Dracula, while
sporting a red badge
on his white breast.

Photographs opposite page:

Upper right: Small village with grocery sign; Khwai

Middle right: Plains zebras, Chapman's race, and wildebeests, western white-bearded race, grazing; Khwai

Lower left: Wildebeests, blue race, walking in open field; Savuti

Photographs this page:

Upper right: Saddle-billed storks, male *(left)* and female, walking; Khwai

Middle right: Male saddle-billed stork, arresting female; Kenya; photograph by Joe McDonald

49

Exposing the Belly

The lions
of my imagining
lurked behind trees,
clandestine,
charging like flying meteors.

How different from
these lounging lions:
flat on their backs,
legs in the air,
paws curled under,
vulnerable
with their bellies exposed.

Watching them was like watching
my cats Isilwane and Ihlosi.
They lay next to each other,
pretending annoyance,
twisting and turning—
the other in the way—
and finally settling in
some mingled position,
irresistible, taking satisfaction
from each other's touch.

Assailable animals.
I could hear the lions purring,
Reach and rub my stomach.

Khwai

Meet Ihlosi of the Bourgognes

First kiss

Repeating Xaxaba

First challenge

First scare

New home

Photographs opposite page:

Upper right: Two lions, lounging; Khwai

Middle right: Two lions, enjoying life and each other; Khwai

Photographs this page:

Upper right: Ihlosi of the Bourgognes; Joyce Williams's yard

Middle right: Ihlosi, confronting Big Cottonwood Creek; Burgoyne backyard

Lower left: Isilwane, intimidating Ihlosi; Burgoyne backyard

Lower middle left: Ihlosi, challenging Isilwane; Burgoyne backyard

Upper middle left: Ihlosi, repeating Xaxaba; Burgoyne backyard

Upper right: Isilwane, greeting Ihlosi for the first time; Burgoyne family room

Isilwane flips and flops
when I brush him; Ihlosi—
she squeals. Both stimulated
by my strokes,
they attack each other.
He tackles; she flips,
jumps straight in the air,
and lands on his back.
Then they sit close,
nose to nose,
eyes wide,
ears back,
paws ready to swat,
before one goes for
the other's neck.

I thought I could
touch these lions—
so seductive,
I believed for a moment
they were tame.
Still, one move toward them,
and they would have killed me.

Khwaí

Ambush

Ihlosi means cheetah; Isilwane means lion.

The Dance

Long-legged solitary giraffes
walk in slow motion,
first both left feet,
then both right.
When they gallop,
forefeet and hind feet
work in pairs.
Their long necks move
in synchrony.
When bulls spar,
they deal blow
and counterblow
with such grace
they seem rather
to dance like
sad lovers
intermingling,
barely moving.

Khwai

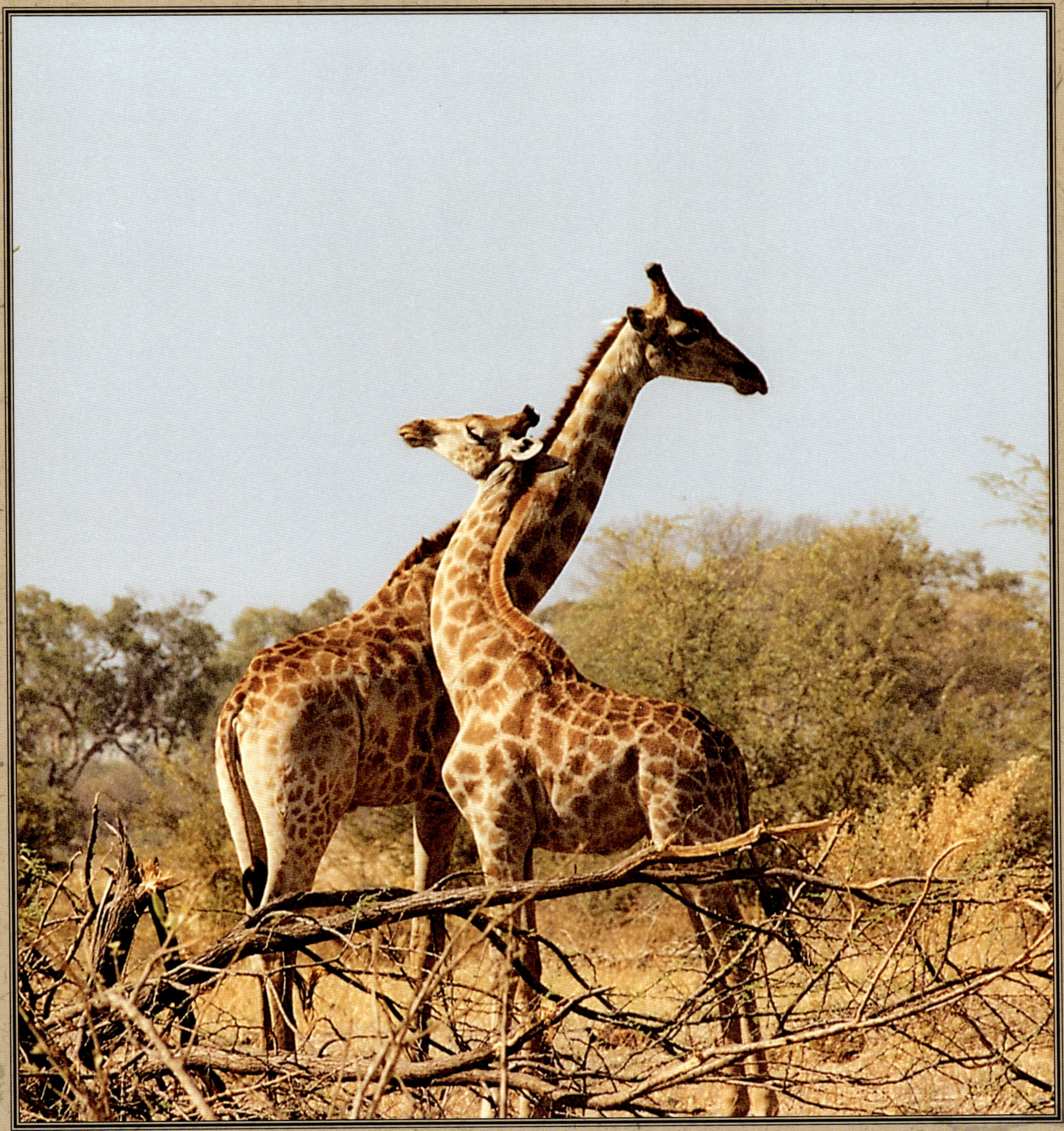

Photographs opposite page:

Upper right: Adult giraffes, Masai race, necking; Hwange

Middle right: Adult giraffes, Masai race, grooming; Hwange

Lower center: Adult giraffes, Masai race, necking; Hwange

Photograph this page:

Feature: Giraffe and young, Masai race, necking; Khwai

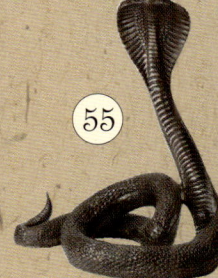

Giraffes' Horns

Both male
and female giraffes
have horns.
From a distance,
you can recognize
who is who
by seniority grazing.
Bulls browse high
and leave regenerating trees
for the females.

At closer glance,
you can tell
males' horns
continue to grow
over the surface
of the skull,
making the head
a knobbed club
by which to gain
breeding dominance.

If those clues
don't help you,
you can hang around
for a mating session.
It's the male
who nudges and butts,
moves the cow gently
with his horns,
resting his head
on her rump
until she stands still
to receive him.

Khwaí

Photographs opposite page:

 *Upper right:* Giraffes, Masai race, eating; Hwange

Middle right: Giraffe, Masai race, eating; Chobe

Photograph this page:

Feature: Male giraffe, Masai race, observing photographer; Chobe

Connections

For three days, Deluxe drove us
across the bridge over the River Khwai
to the Moremi Reserve. The bridge's spiked sides
seemed hardly wide enough to let us pass by.
We'd rumble back and forth across its wooden floor,
hoping each time it would be strong enough
to hold the Land Rover; more fit it seemed
for a walking bridge.

The first day,
we saw all kinds of antelope.
The waterbuck,
lined with white markings,
were easiest to spot:
ear linings, eyebrows,
a ring on their noses,
a bib at their throats,
a bull's eye ring on their rumps.

Khwai

The second day,
once again across the bridge,
we stopped before
two adult males,
not far from a herd of females,
guarding their territory.
Deluxe, nonplussed,
explained males'
rite of passage:
"They begin to compete
for females at age six,
years after maturity.
Their sexual dominance is short—
two, maybe four peak years,
when their possessions
are challenged by
young bachelors
already adept at sneaking matings.
Short but supreme,"
he smiled at me.

Photographs opposite page:

Upper right: Khwai bridge to Moremi Reserve; Khwai

Middle right: Two waterbuck, common race, standing still; Khwai

Photographs this page:

Upper right: Male waterbuck, common race, facing camera; Khwai

Middle right: Waterbuck herd, common race, gathered under tree; Khwai

Lower left: Deluxe, Khwai guide, in camp; Khwai

The third day
across the bridge,
we chanced upon the females.
Deluxe explained their rituals:
"Females return to the same thicket
time and again
to birth their young,
then hide their calves
until the young become
too eager to control.
Calves bolt rather than hide
when frightened by intruders.
These females
keep track of their young
by extending their tails
for their calves to follow.
A sign—unusual."
I looked up curiously at Deluxe.
"Really," he answered.

I should have liked to see the signal,
but by August,
I could barely distinguish
the babies from their mothers.

Khwai

Childless,
I should have liked to
witness this—

My baby cat Ihlosi sucks my neck
each night. When I wake up—
she knows every time I do—
she comes to my face and cries
until I grab her and place her
under my chin. She sucks, kneads
my chest. I hold her claws
so she doesn't hurt so much.
My husband, listening to her
slurps and gurgles, thinks we're
both disgusting, the cat taking
only air from my skin,
her svelte body draped
across the breasts he covets.
But I come close to knowing
a baby's suckle.

I call her my attachment,
feel my instincts surging,
my spirit ascending.

Mothers with white bracelets
on each hoof,
their low bleat calls
as we rumble back across
the wooden floor
of the Khwai bridge.

Photographs opposite page:

Upper right: Female waterbuck herd, common race, huddling by trees; Khwai

Middle right: Female waterbuck herd, common race, grazing; Khwai

Upper left: Madonna and child; carved from a single piece of olive wood; Jerusalem; Burgoyne art collection

Photographs this page:

Upper right: Ihlosi, hiding in ivy; Burgoyne backyard

Middle right: Gardenias, blooming by Tess's grave; Burgoyne backyard

Lower center: Lilies, blooming on Xaxaba's grave; Burgoyne backyard

Middle center: Ihlosi in Marianne's arms, sucking her neck; Burgoyne home

Uppermost center: Female waterbuck, common race, cautious; Khwai

M others with piglets,
 warthogs graze, wary
 of hyenas and leopards.

P oor warthog—breakfast,
 killed by the unseen leopard
 too soon in the spring.

Khwai

Hungry elephant
    eats dry trees at leisure;
      marks us with her sly eye.

Females in estrus,
    baboons mate, taking pleasure
      in naked daylight.

Gentle impala,
    seeking refuge, mourn
      kinsmen brutally taken.

Photographs this page:

Upper right: African elephant, lunching on tree; Khwai

Middle right: Impala, safe in thicket; Khwai

Middle left: Savanna baboons, mating; Khwai

Upper left: Lapis elephant from South Africa;
    Burgoyne jewelry collection

Photographs opposite page:

Upper right: Savanna warthogs and young, grazing; Khwai

Middle right: Poor warthog, dead in a tree; Khwai

Middle left: Malachite from South Africa and lapis
    from China; Burgoyne jewelry collection

63

Elusive

Deep in the Khwai woods,
we saw the leopard—
a fleeting look.
As she walked through dense bush,
it was more that we could see
the leaves quiver
and hear twigs snap,
glimpse a flash of black rosettes.

She was there, skillful cat,
not wanting to be disturbed.
Deluxe had parked the Land Rover
perpendicular
instead of parallel
with the animal.
When the large man in front of me
stood to snap a picture,
he blocked my only chance
to capture her splendor.

Aloof she was, hard to get—
this furtive feline;
her mystery,
I kept thinking,
makes her something
to covet.

She had dragged her kill
up the tree,
cached it on a branch,
unwilling to share her meal
with any but her cubs, hidden
where only she knew.

Subtle, supple,
elusive as the wind
or a dead lover's voice,
this leopard was not for me.
I wanted to be her,
to surrender into her,
to be unattainable, nocturnal,
clandestine. Then I would share
her secrets and dissolve
into her femininity,
and be myself
an intangible mystery.

Khwai

Photographs opposite page:

 Upper right: Leopard cub, resting in tree; Masai Mara, Kenya

 Middle right: Leopard, lying under tree during rainstorm; Masai Mara, Kenya

65

Photograph this page:

Feature: Leopard, resting in tree at sunset; Masai Mara, Kenya

Four Males, a Female, and a Bone

The lions had already made their kill. We couldn't see what they were eating— an antelope? They were down to bare bones. One male, deep in the wood, was by the carcass; he was the bloodiest. A second male was near him; a third, forefront, by the side of the road, chewing on a bone. The fourth male had designs on the female who hadn't eaten. She had designs on the bone. She was the last to eat—something about the great chain of being, but she knew what to do. She inched closer to the bone. They snarled at every movement she made.

First male, deep in wood

Second male

Third male, forefront

Khwai

Fourth amorous male

Fetching female

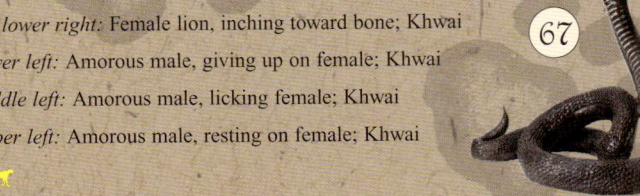

Photographs this page:

🐾 *Upper right:* Fourth male lion, lovesick; Khwai

🐾 *Far middle right:* Fourth male, lovesick and pining; Khwai

🐾 *Middle right:* Female lion—fetching feline; Khwai

🐾 *Far lower right:* Female lion, inching toward bone; Khwai

🐾 *Lower left:* Amorous male, giving up on female; Khwai

🐾 *Middle left:* Amorous male, licking female; Khwai

🐾 *Upper left:* Amorous male, resting on female; Khwai

🐾 🦁

Photographs opposite page:

🐾 *Upper right:* Male lion, deep in wood; Khwai

🐾 *Far middle right:* Male lion by carcass; Khwai

🐾 *Middle-right:* Third male lion, chewing on bone; Khwai

🐾 *Far lower right:* Third male lion, chewing on bone; Khwai

🐾 *Middle left:* Second male, resting; Khwai

🐾 🦁

67

The amorous one began his courtship.
He rested his head on the female's tawny body
and then began licking and coaxing,
making all the right approaches.
She finally presented herself to him,
while aligning herself directly facing the bone.
As he mounted, she moved yet closer
to her desire. During the harsh yowls that followed,
the snarls and growls, she managed—
clever female—to snatch the bone.
Why has she never been given more credit?

Khwai

As she began her feast, the second male came
from the carcass with bloody face and mane.
It was his turn to mate. But the female was
chewing, busy with her meager portion.
He tried to wait patiently; couldn't,
gave a silent roar, demonstrating agony.
Since he is capable of mating 3.5 times an hour,
why shouldn't he be impatient waiting more than
17.14 minutes? It will take her at least that long
to finish the bone.

Photographs this page:

Upper right: Three male lions and a female lion, close to road; Khwai

Middle right: Amorous lion, pining, and female lion, chewing on bone; Khwai

Middle left: Second male lion, coming from woods with bloody mane; Khwai

Photographs opposite page:

Far upper right: Male and female lions, resting; Khwai

Upper right: Male and female lions, resting, and male lion, eating; Khwai

Middle right: Male and female lions, mating, and male lion, disturbed; Khwai

Far lower right: Male lion, mounting female; Khwai

Middle left: Second male and female lion, walking to mate; Khwai

Photographs next page:

Upper right: Two male lions, one in agony, and female lion; Khwai

Middle right: Huts and *boma*; Khwai

Lower left: Cats; Swarovski crystal; Burgoyne art collection

Middle left: Male lion, roaring silently, with female, eating; Khwai

Upper left: Male lion, waiting impatiently to mate with female, eating; Khwai

Khwai

Chobe

Along the Chobe River,
close to the Mowana Safari Lodge,
we spotted a tree boasting
a colony of African darters.

Darting Fishers

Along the Chobe River,
close to the Mowana Safari Lodge,
we spotted a tree boasting
a colony of African darters.
They are like large cormorants
but more elegant.
Their heads are small;
their beaks like harpoons.
Their long-kinked necks curve
with grace into their raven bodies.
Those bodies lengthen into
exquisite fan tails.
They have great heron wings,
so when they fly,
they look like soaring crucifixes
darkening the sky.
These darters,
show-stopping fishers,
spear their catch
and then flip it into the air—
not unlike a cat tossing its prey—
catch it, and swallow it headfirst.
Fish taste better that way.

Chobe

Photographs opposite page:

🦛 *Upper right:* Reed cormorant *(left)* and two African darters, perched on tree; Mowana near Chobe

🦛 *Middle right:* African darters in flight; Mowana near Chobe

🦛 *Lower right:* A2-CHE single-engine Cessna; Khwai to Mowana

🦛 *Uppermost left:* African darter on limb; Mowana near Chobe

Photographs this page:

🦛 *Upper right:* Mowana Safari Lodge along Chobe River; Mowana

🦛 *Middle right:* Mowana tree within safari lodge; Mowana

🦛 *Lower left:* Entrance to Mowana Safari Lodge; Mowana

🦛 *Middle left:* African darter, soaring; Mowana near Chobe

🦛 *Upper left:* Sign—entrance to Chobe National Park; Chobe

mp title page:

Feature: African darter, perched on tree; Mowana near Chobe

emier camp photograph:

▶ *Feature:* Tree, boasting a colony of African darters; Mowana near Chobe

75

Shy, she struts,
stubby legs, rotund body,
jaws too broad to be classic.

Smart hippo, beauty conscious,
makes her own sunblock,
a salve in summer.

Chobe

In sync, single file,
young bulls follow the leader:
eat, drink, bathe, play, mate.

Photographs opposite page:

Upper right: Common hippopotamus, walking along river; Chobe

Middle right: Common hippopotamus, smart and beauty conscious; Chobe

Lower left: Common hippopotamuses, gathered along river; Chobe

Upper left: Common hippopotamus, strolling; Chobe

Photographs this page:

Feature: Young male African elephants in sync, single file; Chobe

Lower left: Wet African elephant, coming out of water; Chobe

Testosterone

Young bull elephants,
too sexually precocious
for their mothers,
become peripheral
to the herd.
I spy them frolicking
together,
submerged in the Chobe,
acting out
mating games on each other.
They play-mate
boisterously
until the sun sleeps.

They must do something
their first twenty-five years,
waiting for the
genuine occurrence,
when they finally
become interesting
to the cows again.
The older they get,
the more preferred
by females,
the more opportunities,
until they drop dead at sixty.

Chobe

Bad Manners

Vultures,
scavengers,
carrion eaters,
shirttailed cousin of the hawk,
dark-plumed, ill-reputed, bad-mannered birds,
you don't have the decency to wait
until your supper is dead.

From our barge on the Chobe,
we watched you at the river's edge
with spur-winged geese and
cattle egrets close by
start feasting on a Cape buffalo wounded.
With your thin, black-tipped bills,
you reached deep for the red muscle
within the dark recesses
of the beast's torn flank.

Perched high, the vulture
spies his next supper—
a rotting, crawling carcass.

Chobe

*C*ape buffalo,

skin split by a lion,

days later; alert, healing.

Photographs opposite page:

Upper right: African buffalo, Cape race, wounded; spur-winged geese and cattle egret close by; Chobe

Middle right: African buffalo, Cape race, dying; spur-winged geese and cattle egret close by; Chobe

Photographs this page:

Feature: African buffalo, Cape race, alert and healing; Chobe

Lower left: White-backed vulture, perched; Chobe

O h, Africa!
    A hundred buffalo roam,
        sanctioned by the Chobe.

B lessed buffalo,
    you lie touching; protect calves
        by charging en masse.

Rare rhinoceros

Chobe

*Crimson queen, perched, sings,
rik, rik, rik; nests, a thousand
pairs in colonies.*

*Snow-white spoonbills snap
at frogs and fish, side-dancing
impala, waterbuck.*

*The pied wagtail chirps,
chiz-zit, chiz-zit; struts across
the bow of our boat.*

Photographs opposite page:

Upper right: African buffalo, Cape race, roaming along river; Chobe

Middle right: African buffalo, Cape race, grazing; Chobe

Middle left: Rare rhinoceros, grazing; South Africa

Photographs this page:

Upper right: Carmine bee-eater, southern race, perched; Chobe

Middle right: African spoonbills among impala and common waterbuck; Chobe

Lower left: African pied wagtail, perched; Chobe

83

Sparring

Bobbing up and down in the Chobe,
male hippopotamuses sparred
with each other, each opening
his huge gape, showing the other
his canine blades and incisor lances,
not to mention the hollow of his throat—
a tunnel to the rotunda of hell.

The guides say most of the time
these males are just playing
unless it's mating season;
they are fighting then
for polygamous dominance.
Their aim—to wound
and conquer.

The hippos remind me of
my husband's polygamous ancestors,
with one difference:
It was the women who fought.
It seems Jonathan Delano
took his wife's sister
for a second wife
without asking Katarina Sabrina
for permission.

Annika Menla was younger
and maybe prettier,
and perhaps J.D. did like her better.
In either case, he housed Katarina
in Montpelier, Idaho
and Annika in Logan, Utah.
State lines and saw-toothed
Beaver Mountain,
impassable in winter,
stood between them.
His strategy was to spend
the winter with the wife he liked better.

Chobe

It was never wise
to put the two women together,
even for a short time.
Annika opened her mouth to speak;
Katarina gritted her teeth.
Their harsh words led
to screaming matches.
J.D. generally intervened
before the pugilism began.
Rumor has it that once
on Main Street, Katarina
grabbed Annika's wrist and bit it.

Worn out at fifty-five, J.D. died first, and
three years later, Annika was buried beside him.
The widow Katarina had thirty more
lonely years to think what to do.
She dug up J.D. and moved him
to the opposite end of the cemetery,
as far away from Annika as she could—
a graveyard of townspeople between them.
When she died, she was placed beside him.

Now, the first cousins, all thirty-eight—
but especially Annika's eight—
think Annika should be moved
to the other side of her legitimate husband.
It's not as easy as it sounds.
Annika has two infant children buried beside her.
She also lies in the corner
with the rest of the Swedish ancestors.
It's Katarina and J.D.
who are at the other end
alone.

At reunions,
the cousins—millionaires and doctors,
lawyers, professors, mothers, and churchmen—
discuss the problems.
They all like each other.

These hippos fighting—
their teeth, spotlighted by the sun, flashing—
I wonder if their domestic traumas
get as complicated as
Jonathan Delano's.
Aiming at the hellish jaws,
I wonder if Jonathan ever thought twice—
Were two wives really better than one?
If it came to that,
would he spar or brawl
to make two sisters perfectly unhappy?

Photographs opposite page:

 *Upper right:* Common hippopotamuses, two sparring; Chobe

Middle right: Common hippopotamuses, resting along bank; Chobe

Photograph this page:

Middle right: Two common hippopotamuses, enlarged, sparring; Chobe

85

The Warriors

Killer took us into Chobe National Park, where we spotted greater kudu bulls hanging out together after mating season. They strode along, confident; their beards hung down long, sturdy throats, distinguishing them from lesser, beardless kudu. They looked like warriors, their faces painted with white chevrons, their tall, narrow bodies with white stripes, making them appear as if they feared no battle. Their crowning glory was their horns, sporting two full turns, which reached toward the sky like giant corkscrews.

Chobe

D oe-eyed, doe-eared female—
not so fierce—licks her newborn;
suckles on demand.

Photographs opposite page:

 *Upper right:* Two male greater kudu, strolling; Chobe

Middle right: Two male greater kudu, framed by tree; Chobe

Middle left: Washbasin in room; Mowana Safari Lodge

Photographs this page:

Upper right: Female greater kudu, eating; Chobe

Middle right: Female greater kudu, eating; Chobe

Lower left: Wine cooler; handmade by Sandy White; Burgoyne art collection

Middle left: Female greater kudu, close-up, eating; Chobe

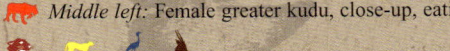

Lion Pride

Deep in the heart of Chobe,
Killer stopped the Land Rover.
A lion pride slept under a tree.
Five—two cubs.
Not much going on;
nice to be lazy.
While we watched,
the little cub in front
awoke and entertained us.
She yawned and licked herself,
sniffed around for someone
to play with, then flopped fast asleep.
She'd just eaten.
Why stress herself?

Chobe

Photographs opposite page:

Upper right: Lion cub, yawning; Chobe

Middle right: Lion cub, licking paw; Chobe

Middle left: Lion cub, grooming; Chobe

Photograph this page:

Feature: Lion pride, sleeping under trees; Chobe

Eyelash Envy

I was born with long lashes;
otherwise, I would be jealous
of those sweeping coverlets
giraffes sport above
ebony eyes.

Nor is any mammal
so graceful.
I took dancing lessons,
or I would be envious of the way
they glide,

so limber, so lissome,
they seem not to touch the earth;
rather, sweep ethereal,
as if through a mist
or dream.

Karen Blixen called them
"elegantly dressed ladies."
Unlike me, they're always
put together perfectly,
always refined.

So womanly,
they appeal—
I won't
apologize—
to my feminine mind.

Chobe

Little Lechwe,

Where are you going
all alone?
Your herd is nowhere,
nor your mother,
nor a crèche of other young.
I suppose back to the swamp—
the reeds, your refuge.
I would have liked
to see you leap and run.

The ugly American in the Land Rover
said, "If you've seen one lechwe,
you've seen them all.
Red, small, greasy critters."
But I should have liked to save you,
to keep the cats from pursuit,
hoping you'd lose them
each time you bounded through water,
haunches lifting you
like a pole vault.

I have read where men in canoes
hold chilas and spear
thousands of you at once.

Lechwe, standing still,
all night, I worried if you
got back with your herd.
I imagined you bounding free,
outrunning wild dogs with ease,
always spirited through the air.

You were special, the only lechwe
we saw close the entire trip.
I claimed you with one glance.
If I could have taken you,
packed you in my sherpa bag—
so no cruel creature
could kill you.

Photographs opposite page:

Upper right: Giraffe, Masai race, with long eyelashes; Chobe

Middle right: Two giraffes, Masai race, nibbling on bush; Chobe

Middle center: Tall giraffe, Masai race, camouflaged by tree; Khwai

Photographs this page:

Upper right: Little lechwe, alone; Chobe

Middle right: Killer—see nametag—and Robert; Chobe

The Kidnapping

I saw a vicious baboon
   steal another female's baby.
The infant had scampered away,
just far enough to get snatched.
Killer said the culprit was a female
who had lost her baby.
During the bedlam which followed,
a big male came to his consort's rescue.
Strutting boldly to the thief, he snatched
the baby and carried it on his back,
returning it to mama. Killer explained
he was likely the godfather, who,
wishing to protect his mating rites,
delivered the little one,
who then clung to its mother's front.
Selfish sexual schemes; intrigue
benefits babies.

Chobe

On guard, the sturdy
savanna baboon sits, watching
over his young.

Monitor lizard
lumbers alone, looking for snails,
birds' nests, tortoises.

Photographs opposite page:

Upper right: Savanna baboon, carrying baby; Chobe

Middle right: Savanna baboon, grooming baby; Chobe

Middle left: Savanna baboon—portrait; Cape Point

Photographs this page:

Upper right: Savanna baboon, Chacma race, male on guard; Chobe

Middle right: Savanna baboon, Chacma race, male on guard; Chobe

Lower center: Young savanna baboons, scampering; Cape Point

Middle left: Savanna monitor lizard, lumbering; Chobe

93

Panic

One lazy afternoon,
a herd of sable antelope
crossed our path.

Chestnut beauties,
their ridged, scimitar horns
burnished by the sun,
led their young
from the forest
to the river.
Sorrel-colored calves
scampered close,
strategically spaced
between their mothers.

Chobe

One calf seemed to be lost.
He bleated louder and louder,
galloped left, then right,
pawed the earth,
bleated louder still,
sniffed the passersby,
until he heard
a low mimiclike call,
his mother's answer.

Photographs opposite page:

Upper right: Sable antelope, leading young to river; Chobe

Middle right: Sable antelope, crossing in front of Land Rover; Chobe

Middle left: Adult sable antelope, walking; Chobe

Photographs this page:

Upper right: Young sable antelope, lost; Chobe

Middle right: Sable antelope herd, drinking along river; Chobe

Lower left: Sable antelope and young, walking to river; Chobe

Middle left: Lost calf, alone; Chobe

At the edge of the Chobe,
the herd circled,
their horns blazing,
the new-found little one
ensconced
within the perimeters.

Chobe

Blaze of Color

The lilac-breasted roller,
a blaze of cinnamon,
turquoise, and purple,
searches for insects
from low perches
in the heat of day.

The roller thrives in
the wildlife reserves.
He seemed to follow us
everywhere we were,
a quick flash darting
from tree to earth,
calling rak-rak
deep in wooded
acacia savannas.

Beautiful bird,
when I came home,
I dreamed you came calling,
your whirl of hues
adding magnificence,
perched on a quaking aspen
in my backyard.

Photographs opposite page:

Upper right: Sable antelope herd, walking along river; Chobe

Middle right: Sable antelope herd, circled together; Chobe

Middle left: Sable antelope with scimitar horns; Chobe

Photographs this page:

Upper right: Lilac-breasted roller, perched; Chobe

Middle right: Lilac-breasted roller, blaze of color; Chobe

Lower center: Lilac-breasted roller, spying the river; Chobe

97

Chobe Pirates

Perched on his lofty branch,
the African fish eagle eyes
the water's glass,
ready for breakfast.
He swishes,
feet extended forward;
one or two large fish
just below the surface will do.
A pirate at heart,
he might even steal a catch or two
from fellow herons or kingfishers,
storks or pelicans.

He soars over African rivers,
often with his female,
whose piercing yelps
call to him
from the water's edge.
She entices;
he acquiesces.
They fly mornings
over their territory,
a splendid duet
maneuvering in unison,
exuberant, flying high.

Chobe

Photographs opposite page:

 *Upper right:* African fish eagle, perched above river; Chobe

 *Middle right:* African fish eagle, perched above river, close-up; Chobe

 *Middle center:* African fish eagle, perched on pole; Chobe

Photograph this page:

 *Feature:* African fish eagle, perched by leaves; Chobe

Survival

You, little crocodile,
your body covered
with horny,
keeled, and bony plates,
seeking refuge on
a miniature island,
have nothing to fear.
Most other creatures
are afraid you will eat them,
even buffalo and zebras.
Your carnage of antelope
is well publicized.
Only the cats, I suppose,
can make a getaway,
outrunning you on land,
quick though you are.

Still, you look lonely,
a bit dreary,
having survived centuries,
your fathers contemporary
with dinosaurs.
What tactics did you have that
they didn't, that you would live
to verify the secrets of survival?
The scholars say
your mother endures
a ninety-day fast,
defending your egg site,
buried in sand,
then carries you in her mouth
and washes you in the river—
a baptism—for you to persevere.

Chobe

Role Reversals

The myth says
the male African jacana
is a ten-legged bird.
Not so.
The truth is—
and this is the truth—
the male incubates the eggs
and carries his four little ones
in an underwing pouch.
The females are busy gathering males
and laying eggs for each of their nests.

The ten legs are real.
When the father goes flying
with his little ones,
flying low over water lilies
and floating hyacinths,
dangling under his wing,
you can see
his long gray legs
and theirs
and everyone's
long toes.

 **Photograph opposite page:**

Feature: Young Nile crocodile near island in river; Chobe

Photographs this page:

Feature: African jacana with reflection in river; Chobe

Lower left: African jacana near water; Lake Kariba

Close

The trick is to get
as close as possible
to the animals
without getting killed—
the higher the risk,
the better the photograph.

So with the crocodile,
we tracked
until he slithered onshore.
I stood up,
crawled on the bow
of the boat,
and looked straight into
his reptile face.
Uncooperative,
he remained expressionless
until I started to move
back to the deck.
With my back turned,
he opened his jaws.
My husband grabbed my hand,
pulled me down,
as we found it necessary
to save ourselves.

Chobe

Photographs opposite page:

 Upper right: Nile crocodile, swimming in river; Chobe

 Middle right: Nile crocodile, slithering onshore; Chobe

Photograph this page:

 Feature: Nile crocodile, close-up and scary; Chobe

103

Next, Sam, our river guide,
pulled the speedboat
into a little inlet.
There stood a Cape buffalo,
guarding his herd.
He stared,
then decided he didn't like us.
He stamped his hoof,
moved his horns from side to side,
snorted, pawed the earth.
The engine choked;
my heart stopped.
Sam put the control in reverse
and whispered,
"Let's get out of here."
"Good idea."
The engine died.
Eternity.
I couldn't speak;
watched Sam pull the starter cord—
the shrill, our jolt backwards,
the bull by now at the water's edge.

Chobe

"How many years did I lose?"
I was about to ask,
when my husband,
terrified, managed,
"Isn't that a hippo up ahead?"
"Where? I believe it is,"
Sam whispered,
as the boat skimmed
over the hippo's head.

"I could be fined for that"
was all Sam said.

Photographs opposite page:

 Upper right: African buffalo, Cape race, angry; Chobe

Middle right: Common hippopotamuses, resting along bank; Chobe

Uppermost left: African buffalo, Cape race, guarding herd; Chobe

Photographs this page:

Upper right: Common hippopotamuses, sparring; Chobe

Middle right: Marianne and Sam, Chobe guide, excursion survivors; Chobe

Middle left: Common hippopotamuses, sparring; Chobe

Mystic

I've always liked marabou storks.
They work along the Chobe shoreline
building nests of sticks and reeds.

Two or three eggs there; the black-winged,
white-bellied birds, mottled heads
red and black, pink necks—not so
beautiful, although their feathers make
hats or stoles in Zhivago white—
their wings the rival of the largest albatross.

In my idyll, they are like the ibis
rare, like the phoenix mystic. And so,
this casual performance of domestic chores—
astonishing.

Chobe

Incorrigible Trunk

Elephants' trunks are used for everything: eating, drinking, bathing. Mothers use theirs to steer their young. Courting elephants twine their trunks. Bulls track female reproductive status. Trumpeting. The list goes on.

So imagine the frustration of a calf whose trunk won't cooperate. He wallows in the water trying to drink. He moves one way; it another. It wiggles and waggles and dangles. It just won't do what he wants it to.

Small comfort when he puts his trunk into his mother's mouth, sometimes to eat, sometimes for reassurance, and even as a greeting. But for now, he must wrestle with its incorrigibility, slow to maneuver its capabilities.

Photographs opposite page:

Upper right: Marabou storks, building nest; Chobe

Middle right: Marabou storks, building nest, close-up; Chobe

Middle left: Marabou storks, building nest, close-up; Chobe

Photographs this page:

Upper right: Baby African elephant, trying to drink; Chobe

Middle right: Baby African elephant, drinking; Chobe

Middle center: Baby African elephant, managing trunk; Chobe

107

The Bond Groups

Along the Chobe River,
we spend the afternoon
watching a large herd
of elephants.

The matriarch,
dictating the day's activities,
bathes the babies,
while a female coalition
of aunts and nieces
joins in scrubbing the youngest.

Chobe

Photographs opposite page:

Upper right: Male African elephant, following herd, secreting musth; Chobe

Middle right: Adult and young African elephants, bathing baby; Chobe

Middle center: Elephant hair necklace and earrings from Cape Town; Burgoyne jewelry collection

Photograph this page:

Feature: Adult and young African elephants, bathing baby; Chobe

Magnificent maternal creatures:
They suckle each other's young.
If one of their own is hurt,
they watch and stay close
or help her to her feet.

Killer, our guide,
interrupts our reveries:
"The government is deciding
whether or no to check
the elephant population
by shooting them."
Sickened, I ask why.
"Because they number
a hundred thousand.
They are eating our forests,
destroying nature's balance
for other animals."
He adds the coup de grâce.
"If you're going to kill them,
you must kill the entire herd
because they are so closely bonded.
If they lose one of their own,
they become mean, even mad,
more of a threat to humans."

Chobe

Later, that night,
I kept thinking of the herd,
babies tucked safely
under their mothers,
so peaceful
at sunset
along the Chobe.

I had seen
the ravaged forests,
the elephants' continual plunder,
and the government's dream
of control
at the point
of a gun.

Photographs opposite page:

Upper right: Adult female African elephant with young; Chobe

Middle right: Adult female African elephants with young, one calf nursing; Chobe

Photographs this page:

Upper right: African elephants with young, tucked safely within herd; Chobe

Middle right: Female African elephant with young, tucked under trunk; Chobe

Middle left: Female African elephant with young, safe under trunk; Chobe

The sun sets on the Chobe;
bond groups bathe serene
in sun-kissed water.

Chobe

The Lone Boatman

The lone boatman
paddles his handcrafted canoe
slowly, perilously,
up the Chobe.
He does not think so;
he is fishing.
He thinks nothing of the dangers
that frighten tourists.
He knows hippopotamuses are territorial.
Knowing where they are,
he avoids them.
The crocodiles' whereabouts
he's not so sure of.
But he's not one to mistake
the reptile for a floating log.
This man has been fishing
the river all his life.
One day, he may not be lucky
and will die here.
Today, he is probably thinking
our motorboat is
disturbing his livelihood;
as importantly, his solitude.

Photograph opposite page:

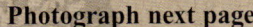 *Feature:* African elephants, drinking at sunset in river; Chobe

Photograph this page:

Feature: Lone boatman, paddling his handcrafted canoe; Chobe

Photograph next page:

Feature: The sun sleeps on the Chobe.

The sun sleeps.

Chobe

Victoria
Falls

David Livingstone lies in Westminster Abbey,
    I presume, because he found Africa for England.

Mosi-oa-Tunya

Smoke That Thunders

David Livingstone lies
in Westminster Abbey,
I presume, because he
found Africa for England.

His heart, I know, lies
in Africa, buried beneath
the tree where he died.
His heart was always there,
since his first days
when he brought medicine
and God. He traveled to regions
where no European had ever been:

the Kalahari Desert, Lake Ngami,
the Zambezi River. Of all the sites
Livingstone happened upon,
none could have been so splendid as
the majestic falls, Mosi-oa-Tunya,
"Smoke That Thunders,"
he named in honor
of his Queen Victoria.

Searching for the mouth
of the Zambezi River,
he stumbled upon
the abrupt descent,
cataracts tumbling four hundred feet,
thirty million tons of water an hour,
to frantic, swirling rainbows of
whirlpools below.

Victoria Falls

Camp title page:

🐘 *Feature:* Victoria Falls, April; border between Zimbabwe and Zambia

Premier camp photograph:

🐘 *Feature:* Zambezi River and Victoria Falls, April; border between Zimbabwe and Zambia

Background photograph for Victoria Falls section, pages 118 through 138:

🐘 *Background:* Chasm, April; Victoria Falls

Photographs opposite page:

🐘 *Upper right:* Zambezi River and chasm, April; Victoria Falls

🐘 *Middle right:* Chasm, April; Victoria Falls

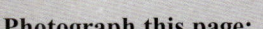

Photograph this page:

🐘 *Feature:* Chasm by helicopter, April; Victoria Falls

119

Five hundred thousand years ago,
when the cold Zambezi cut
across basaltic rock
and swaths of softer sandstone,
different rates of erosion,
hard caprock plunging
to fathomless depths,
the cataracts carved themselves.

I have read that
the Kololo people of the West
avoided them, fearing evil.
The Tonga tribe
thought them sacred,
making live animal sacrifices,
plunging lechwe headlong
to their deaths.

Monsoon waters tumble;
steam rises from the abyss.
I stand alongside Devil's Cataract,
where Livingstone stood, drenched,
all but obliterated by the roar,
the vapor, the rumble, the crash,
explorer discovering the force
of God—ineffable, immutable.

Victoria Falls

Photographs opposite page:

 *Upper right:* Zambezi River to Devil's Cataract, April; Victoria Falls

Middle right: Chasm from rain forest, April; Victoria Falls

Photograph this page:

Feature: Devil's Cataract from rain forest, August; Victoria Falls

The Little Rain Forest
Victoria Falls National Park

We walk along
a tiny path,
ensconced by trees
too tall to end,
finding ourselves
lost in an exotic maze
of ilala palms and ebonies,
canopies above canopies
of fig trees topped
by mahoganies,
shading broadleaf ferns
in dense abundance,
and finally, blood lilies
covering the earth.
Vertical layers of foliage,
like leaves stacked in a book,
stretch from floor to sky,
rendering it impossible
to see the sun.

It always rains here
opposite Victoria Falls.
I walk along,
flirting with the abyss,
not so afraid now,
having decades ago
taken my fall,
raindrops
splashing my face,
my blouse soaked,
sticking to my skin—
all this
mitigating water!

Victoria Falls

Photographs opposite page:

Upper right: Rain forest across from Devil's Cataract, August; Victoria Falls National Park

Middle right: Rain forest with falls in background, August; Victoria Falls National Park

Lower center: Sign; Victoria Falls

Photograph this page:

Feature: Trees too tall to end with trumpeter hornbill, perched, August; Victoria Falls National Park

I feel wildly happy,
as happy as the day
a decade ago
when we climbed
the Great Wall.
Recovered
from a three-year illness,
speaking French to Frenchmen
who praised my diction,
counting from one to ten
in Chinese,
surrounded by a sea
of black-haired women
pointing at my Blahnik sandals,
shedding layers of
condemnation,
I felt a logarithmic rise
from perdition
to the other side
of the chasm.

Here,
at the end of
this little rain forest,
I look down at the
Boiling Pot below,
the mist
familiar,
rising
like Hades,
still not high enough
to reach me.
I pluck a blood lily
from the earth,
turn to my Orpheus,
willing to return to hell,
seventy-times-seven
times willing
to save me.

Victoria Falls

Photographs opposite page:

Upper right: Marianne, leaning on the Great Wall; China 1987

Middle right: Boiling Pot at end of walking tour, August; Victoria Falls

Photograph this page:

Feature: Chasm, leading to Boiling Pot, August; Victoria Falls

125

The French Bath

My husband has never taken me camping—
"The bath," he says, "is too heavy to cart."
We've slept outside on our balcony twice
in twenty-seven years.

So journeying to Africa,
staying in safari camps,
presented a slight dilemma.
When my best friend asked,
"What on earth will you wear?"
and I answered, "White linen suits
and lace-up boots," she rolled her eyes
and perhaps said a silent prayer.

I admit, this was the luxury tour,
the camps run by Orient Express Hotels.
But at Khwai, the shower stall
was rough-hewn cement,
and I snuck in with the spiders—
watched them every second.
Water trickled from the spout—cold
at 6:00 a.m., drizzling down my soapy hair.
Not compromising well,
I endured the ordeal
every morning.

Victoria Falls

The Victoria Falls Hotel—
nineteenth-century elegance
of a bygone era,
columns and marble floors,
labyrinthine hallways,
circular staircases, pictures
of Queen Victoria and young Elizabeth
on the walls—wistful—
is the fanciest place
I have yet laid my head.
After huts with thatched roofs
filled with bugs—
now wood-carved beds
and white linens,
a gossamer mosquito net
draped like a bridal veil
over our heads,

Photographs opposite page:

Upper right: Marianne, posing; Hwange Airport

Middle right: Entrance to Victoria Falls Hotel; Victoria Falls

Lower center: Sign; Victoria Falls

Photographs this page:

Upper right: Marianne, climbing circular staircase; Victoria Falls Hotel

Middle right: Robert, coming from labyrinthine hallway; Victoria Falls Hotel

Lower left: Bed, draped with mosquito net; Victoria Falls Hotel

and splendid!
an old-fashioned
French bath with legs, a nozzle,
and jasmine bubble bath.

So I bathed my usual
three times a day,
between morning and afternoon safaris,
and if it was easier
to stand in the separate shower,
I'd hop out and wash my hair there,
returning to soak with mud on my face
and conditioner on my hair.
My husband says I am
the sensitive princess with
the proverbial pea.
I don't care. I enjoy myself.

Victoria Falls

And later,
when we dined
in the grand ballroom,
black tie, dancing to a British combo,
I, in my one silk dress packed within
my twenty-five-pound luggage allotment;
I, raised in a girl's boarding school,
trained in manners and etiquette,
couldn't name two of the pieces
of the full place setting or
all the silver that matched it.

Photographs opposite page:

Upper right: Room; Victoria Falls Hotel

Middle right: The French bath; Victoria Falls Hotel

Lower left: Splendid sink; Victoria Falls Hotel

Photographs this page:

Upper right: Back patio; Victoria Falls Hotel

Middle right: Patio outside dining room; Victoria Falls Hotel

Middle left: Juliet, 1987; bronze by Victor Villarreal, twelve of twenty;
    Mexico; Burgoyne art collection

129

The Canoe Ride

Canoeing the Zambezi at sunset is something the tourists do because David Livingstone did it and lived to write about this "Crimson Heart of Africa bleeding over the Kandahar Rapids."

Deadly—
should you brave
its sinuous course,
you gamble safety for treachery,
sanity for forgotten prayers.
That is why it is so alluring.
The river will not wait for you.
You must decide how brave,
how willing your heart's surrender.

Victoria Falls

Gabriel,
the head guide, said,
"Canoeing the Zambezi
is not without peril. We ask
you to sign an indemnity:
name, address, and next of kin."
Then he said, "We must discuss
Plan A and Plan B.
Plan A: If the hippo comes
up under the canoe, chances are
he will bounce you up,
and you will land
back in the canoe.
Plan B: If he capsizes the canoe,
your job is to swim as far away
as possible because he will try
to reattack the canoe."

By this time, all eleven of us
were thinking there were better ways
to spend the afternoon.
One of us asked,
"What about Plan C?"
"Plan C. Plan C—we never
discuss it unless it happens,
at which time, the six of us
will try to save all eleven of you."

Besides the hippos,
the crocodiles have been known
to snatch the boatmen,
and if those two don't get you,
the parasites will. Should you
fall in the water,
they infiltrate your ears.
You are dead in two weeks.

Gabriel

Photographs opposite page:

🐆 *Upper right:* Canoe group and barge, setting out; Zambezi River

🐆 *Middle right:* Canoe with guide, paddling upstream; Zambezi River

🐆 *Lower right:* Guide and fellow passengers, braving dangers; Zambezi River

🐆 *Middle center:* Sign, pointing to Zambezi River; Victoria Falls

🐆 *Uppermost left:* "Crimson Heart of Africa"; Zambezi River

Photographs this page:

🐆 *Upper right:* Guides on canoe safari; Zambezi River

🐆 *Middle right:* Fellow tourists and Robert *(right),* braving canoe ride; Zambezi River

🐆 *Uppermost center:* Our guide Gabriel; Zambezi River

131

"One last warning,"
continued Gabriel.
"Don't put one leg, one knee,
one arm, one finger
out of the canoe or
otherwise call attention
to yourself. Just sit back
and enjoy the trip;
we do all the work."

The first crocodile
was only a baby,
sunning himself on a
river branch.
Such a miniature,
he seemed no danger;
not so his counterpart,
lurking in reeds
at the river's edge.
Crocodiles move fast
if they decide to;
we backpaddled away
and steered clear of others,
their eyes staring at us,
and of the hippos sleeping
along the bank.
It's possible to take this trip
because the guides
know what to do.

Victoria Falls

We watched for a time
an African open-billed stork
feeding on freshwater snails
and mussels, the open gap
toward the tip of his beak
adapted to crack their shells.
Breathtaking
when he took wing,
off to land on some hippo's back
as they sometimes do.
The chestnut African jacana
feeds from the backs of hippos,
or, with delicate legs and toes,
turns over the undersides
of water lilies
to hunt for insects.

So splendid at sundown,
the sundowner route,
the sky turning
melon, then crimson
as Livingstone said,
birds hovering overhead,
it is easy to forget
the dangers even though
we head for shore,
the water racing faster
one kilometer before
Devil's Cataract
at Victoria Falls.

Victoria Falls

Photographs opposite page:

Upper right: Sun, turning melon, then crimson; Zambezi River

Middle right: Canoe safari, heading toward Devil's Cataract; Zambezi River

Middle left: Marianne and Robert on break across Zambezi River; photograph by head guide

Middle center: Black ravens in flight; Zambezi River

Uppermost left: African open-billed stork in flight; Zambezi River.

Photograph this page:

Feature: Drop-off of Devil's Cataract, August; Zambezi River

135

Real Baobabs

When I read
The Little Prince,
I thought baobab trees
were make-believe.
I had not yet been to Africa.
I now see them
as uncultivated and
numerous as termite mounds,
rising like chimneys
or drooping like mushrooms.
Not the catastrophe
the prince thought them to be,
their thick trunks
and tall limbs sprawling
outward and upward
add stark majesty—giant
scarecrows rooted in primal soil.

I have traveled this far
from my world.
No roses grow for me to tame.

Victoria Falls

C raft Village replicas,
      circled huts within huts,
         grass dwellings of kings.

Photographs opposite page:

🐘 *Upper right:* Baobab tree near Zambezi River; Victoria Falls

🐘 *Middle right:* Rhodes Bridge, named after Cecil John, with bungee jumper; Victoria Falls

🐾 🐆

Photographs this page:

🐘 *Upper right:* Craft Village huts, replicas; Victoria Falls

🐘 *Middle right:* Grass huts; large replica of king's dwelling; Victoria Falls

🐊 *Lower left:* Wooden giraffe head; hand carved in Kenya

🐊 *Middle center:* Wooden cheetah head; hand carved in Kenya

🐊 *Middle left:* Wooden zebra head; hand carved in Kenya

🐾 🐆

Photographs next page:

🐘 *Upper right:* Helicopter in flight; Victoria Falls

🐘 *Feature:* Chasm, September; Victoria Falls

Natural Wonder
by Helicopter

Lifting from the helicopter launch,
     I, seated beside the pilot,
side window open,
could see the steam rising,
ready with my camera
to click Victoria Falls,
determined,
scared to death—
my second helicopter ride.

Years before in China,
I was told astronauts
can see the Grand Canyon
and the Great Wall
with the naked eye.
As we circled,
I felt like an astronaut gazing—
thrilling to view
the extent of the chasm—
a mile wide.

Monsoon rains thunder.
Rainbows glisten.
I, John Glenn, circling,
by now far above the chasm,
realize how close our canoe ride
took us to the verge of disaster.
A rush of blood—my joy surges.
I align with this power—
this one omnispective glimpse.

Victoria Falls

Hwange

Meet Ma

At Jijima, the private camp on the fringe

e Kalahari sand in Zimbabwe near Hwange...,

The Private Camp

At Jijima,
the private camp
on the fringe
of the Kalahari sand
in Zimbabwe
near Hwange,
Zimbabwe's largest national park,
we asked our guide Dean,
a bushman since birth,
if Michelle
was married to Ron,
the owner.
"No," Dean said.
"Ron's wife died
two years ago—
quite tragically,
actually.
It seems she had
to make a choice.
She was driving
to the airport
when she realized
a cobra was
in the car
with her.
It was either
the cobra
or jump.
She chose to jump.
The car ran her over."

Hwange

Dean tells us
she lingered
a month or two.
I waited a day
to present my condolences.
Then Lady Diana died.
News came to Ron's camp
two and a half days late.
We all sat sober
that night by the campfire,
when, seated at Ron's right,
I said, "I'm sorry about your wife."
"So am I.
But then,
nothing survives long
in Africa."

It was a phrase
I will not forget.
I watched Ron struggle
to keep his pet impala alive.
"Yes," he said, "both lions
and wild dogs have attacked
her right here in the camp.
When the four lions attacked,
she disappeared for so long,
I thought she was gone.
But then, she came and stood
at the edge of the camp,
afraid to come back.
I fed her cornflakes
for nine days
until she slowly inched her way
back to my tent.
It's just a matter of time
with her."

Camp title page:

Feature: Ma, Ron's pet impala; Jijima

Premier camp photograph:

Feature: Ron's private camp with Ma, resting; Jijima

Photographs opposite page:

Upper right: Colin, Michelle, and Ron, reluctant posers; Jijima

Middle right: Ron's private camp, April; Jijima

Photographs this page:

Uppermost right: Sign; Isilwane means *lion*; Jijima

Upper right: Ma with Dean on walk break; Jijima

Middle right: Rod with Ma in camp, April; Jijima

Uppermost center: Our particular hut, named Isilwane; Jijima

143

During our three days here,
I heard Ron say it again and again:
"It's just a matter of time,
a matter of time. Nothing
survives long in Africa."

Before I came home,
I didn't buy a stuffed impala.
I bought a bronze cobra instead,
coiled,
ready to strike,
and later,
at home,
placed him
at the entrance
to my living room.

Hwange

Meet Ma

Ron's pet impala, the little female found in the bush—her mother killed by lions—was only weeks old when Ron found her. She said, Ma, Ma, terrified of the stranger. Ron brought her to the camp where she is now the star of the resort. She eats cornflakes for breakfast and sleeps outside our tent because she likes us.

The guides all look after her. Ron says they will lose their jobs if they don't. So Dean was a bit put out when she followed us on our walk. He scolded her, threw rocks her way, shooed her home, but she just kept trotting behind us. Ma likes Dean. It's just that after we had walked several miles, we all rode home, except him and Ma. She won't come near the Land Rover. So Dean had to march her back to camp.

Photographs opposite page:

Upper right: Marianne and other tourists, following Dean on walk; Jijima

Far upper right: Bronze cobra; purchased in Cape Town; Burgoyne art collection

Middle right: Boma and patio; Jijima

Lower left: Male ostrich, Somali race, walking; Hwange

Middle center: Ma, following Dean and other tourists on walk; Jijima

Upper center: Marianne and other tourists, following Dean; Jijima

Photographs this page:

Upper right: Marianne, coaxing Ma; Jijima

Middle right: Dean, rubbing Ma's nose; Jijima

Lower left: Ma, going for the cornflakes of British tourist; Jijima

145

After we had finished lunch, here they came,
Dean exhausted from the double run,
and Ma looking fit enough to try it all again.

At dinner, Ron talks about getting lost
deep in the Okavango.
"The waterways all look alike.
We find ourselves circling until
it seems we will never find our way out.
I tell you, it's a maze out there."

By the late campfire, I am overwhelmed.
It is so dark. At 9:59 p.m., the camp's
gas lanterns are shut out. So remote are we—
no telephones—the Morse code isn't working.
Is my mother alive?
I am a long way from Ferron.

I hear conversations around me,
the crack of the fire, the chill punctuated
by a distant howl. How far away from peril?
Did my aunt survive pneumonia?
I like when Ma lies at my feet.
I want her close.

It is this night in a tunnel in France
that Diana never makes it back to England.

Hwange

I fear for Ma,
her slim face and elegant nose.
All animals remind me of my own.

It was last February when
the veterinarian called
and said Tess had lymphoma.
The next morning, we canceled
our April trip to Africa.
Chemotherapy cured the cancer,
but her kidneys failed in June.

We buried her in cedar
just to the side of the white birch—
cedar because
it might keep her near
my last forty years.

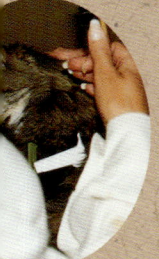

I sleep in the same single bed with my husband.
But I lie awake thinking something
is wrong—the world riveted
by a woman dying, whispering
she has a baby in her belly.

I hear a cry. I get up, unzip my tent,
and see Ma sleeping outside Ron's bungalow.

A star falls.
Ron is right. Nothing survives
long…and always, some unseen thing
comes in the night to take us.

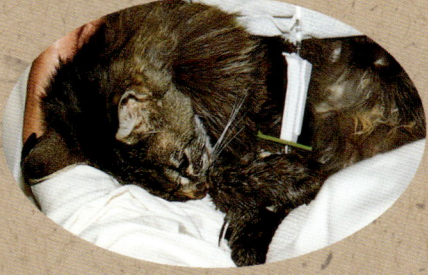

Photographs opposite page:

🐾 *Upper right:* Ma outside our Isilwane tent; Jijima

🐾 *Middle right:* Dean, Australian tourists, and Ma, scheming to join walk; Jijima

🐾 *Uppermost left:* Ma, posing; Jijima

Photographs this page:

🐘 *Upper right:* Ma, greeting Marianne; Jijima

🐾 *Middle right:* Robert and Brad Christensen, placing Tess's coffin in the earth; Burgoyne backyard

🐾 *Lower center:* Tess, two days before she died; Burgoyne backyard

🐘 *Lowermost left:* Tess in Marianne's arms, one day before she died; Cottonwood Animal Hospital

🐘 *Far middle left:* Tess in Marianne's arms, one day before she died; Cottonwood Animal Hospital

🐘 *Far upper left:* Tess in Marianne's arms, one day before she died; Cottonwood Animal Hospital

🐾 *Uppermost left:* Ma outside our bungalow; Jijima

147

The Thinker

Sits contemplating
life's mysteries:
availability
of food, water,
sleeping sites.
Troop rank,
dominance,
mating rites.
Consort status,
godfather privileges,
grooming rank.

I like to watch
these social creatures,
emotions flickering
across expressive faces.

Although
the alpha male
gets a greater share
of estrous females,
the thinker is surprisingly
not jealous.
Females present
themselves anyway,
enhancing his own performance.

Hwange

The Baboon Scratcher

When a baby baboon
doesn't know what to do,
he scratches his behind.
He thinks we're strange,
stares at us all the same,
and stays close to his mother.
Animals are rarely embarrassed,
and in that way, smarter than we.

Baby baboons, safe,
eat buds hand to mouth,
sheltered by doting mothers.

Photographs opposite page:

Upper right: The thinker, inspiration from Rodin; savanna baboon, yellow race; Hwange

Middle right: The thinker, contemplating mating rites; savanna baboon, yellow race; Hwange

Photographs this page:

Upper right: Young savanna baboon, yellow race, scratching behind; Hwange

Middle right: Adult and young savanna baboons, yellow race, eating; Hwange

Lower left: Drum; handcrafted in Ghana

Middle left: Small drum, replica; handcrafted in Ghana

149

Flat Tires

As I said,
Pijima, a private camp,
located on the eastern boundary
of Hwange National Park,
is primitive. Although
it was the only camp where we found
hot-water bottles in the bed,
they were most needed there.
The edge of the Kalahari
is cold at night.

It shouldn't have been surprising
we had three flat tires in two days.
It's just that breaking down
with wild animals all around
gave us something to think about.
We'd all hop out of the Toyota;
the men would go to work.
Particularly at night, we'd see
eyes peering at us, fluorescent,
from the midnight beyond.

Of course, it got to be funny.
Amazing, there was always
a workable spare. I didn't dare
contemplate how chilling the
walk would have been otherwise.
If we had chanced upon
any animal besides a hare,
the scare would have killed us.

Hwange

The guides never carry a gun
in these protected parks
and rightly so. This way,
there are no accidents. Even so,
the cheetahs could have bested us.
Probably even the baboons.

Earlier that day, we had been chased
by an elephant, his powerful legs
beginning in slow motion until Dean
stopped a full charge by pounding
on his door. The bull stopped,
then circled round behind us,
ready to charge again. I thought it
was forever before our wheels
started to spin in the Kalahari sand.

Photographs this page:

Upper right: British and Australian tourists, Robert, and Dean, fixing tire; Hwange

Middle right: African elephant, blocking road, and later, charging; Hwange

Lower left: Acacia umbrella thorn tree in park; Hwange

Middle left: African elephant, just before charging; Hwange

Photographs opposite page:

Upper right: Robert, Dean, and Australian tourists after flat-tire break; Hwange

Middle right: Robert, Dean, and tourists, fixing flat tire; Hwange

Lower middle center: Common duiker, camouflaged by night; Hwange

Upper middle center: Common duiker, bounding away; Hwange

Photographs next page:

Upper right: African wild dog, ambling; Hwange

Far middle right: African wild dog, patchwork mutt; Hwange

Middle right: Four African wild dogs, moving on; Hwange

Lower center: Dean, expounding on animal droppings; Hwange

Killers

Wild dogs,
patchwork mutts,
never favorites,
never welcome visitors.
Once striking
a particular turf—
and again and once again—
the gazelles, the warthogs, the zebras
abandon it. So the
dogs wander.

We saw four critters,
heartless killers,
ambling near Jijima.
Dean said he hadn't
seen them in these parts
for five months.
They had just rent
the belly of
a wildebeest calf
and gorged upon
the entrails; now
were moving on.

Hwange

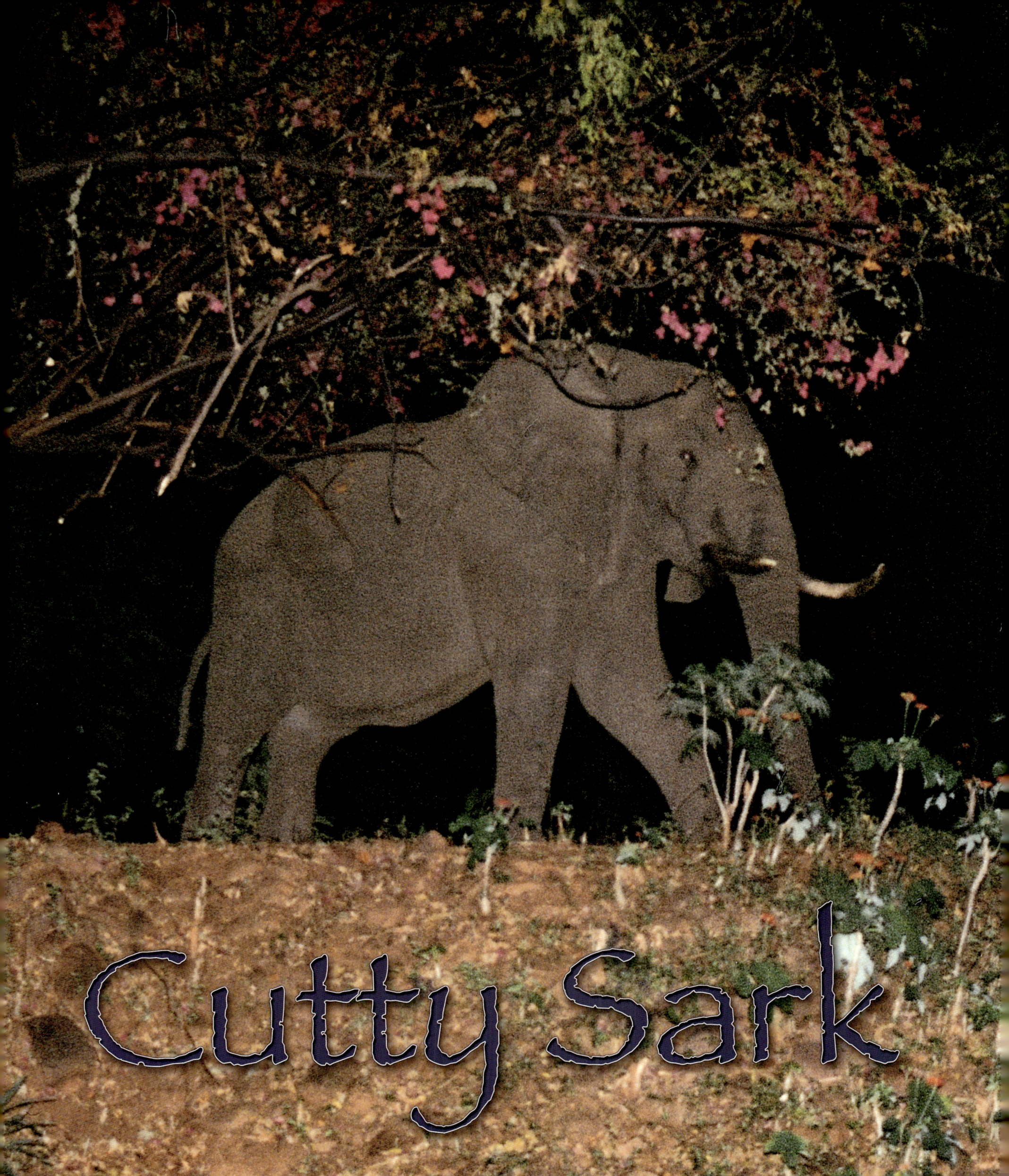

Cutty Sark

Air Zimbabwe is never on time.
Sometimes the planes don't show up at all.

Unexpected Stop

Air Zimbabwe is never on time.
Sometimes the planes don't show up at all.
This is because the plane that is used to fly
the tourists also flies the president.
If he needs the plane, so be it.

We were supposed to travel from Jijima
to Fothergill Island Lodge on Lake Kariba,
but the plane was three hours late.
We missed the last ferry. Instead,
we were whisked to the Cutty Sark Hotel.

After dinner, the waiters said
we couldn't return to our room
the same way we had come.
The largest elephants I had to date seen
were taking their meals from the landscaped trees.

This made the establishment mad.
The big guys were ruining the premises.
The waiters banged on pans,
shooed at them, but to no avail.
They were hungry.

We walked back to our room
by way of the swimming pool and
snapped pictures from the balcony.
Two elephants spent most of the night
ten feet away from our doorway.

Hearing branches crack and snap,
I wondered if the hotel walls were edible.
I dreamed the recurring nightmare
of my childhood: a heavy weight
upon me, suffocating.

Cutty Sark

Night Terrors

In the night
when the terrors come—
   elephants stampeding have
   trampled my brother;
   my father speaks;
   sharks circle my
   unsafe feet;
   I am the only one unmarried;
   the illicit slams
   face forward;
   I am too late
   to escape the usual
   labyrinths;
   in a classroom crying,
   taking a test for which
   there was never a text;
   all weigh
   like a heavy man
   upon a child—
my mind awakes
to find your serene face;
I hear you saying,
"No harm, no harm."

Camp title page:

🐘 *Feature:* African elephant outside hotel room; Cutty Sark

Premier camp photograph:

🐘 *Feature:* African elephant, approaching stairway to hotel rooms; Cutty Sark

Photographs opposite page:

🐘 *Uppermost right:* Air Zimbabwe, A2-ABD; Harare to Cutty Sark

🐘 *Upper right:* Marianne, waiting to board Air Zimbabwe; Harare

🐘 *Middle right:* African elephant at top of hotel stairway; Cutty Sark Hotel

🐘 *Middle center:* African elephant, ten feet away from room; Cutty Sark Hotel

Photographs this page:

🐘 *Upper right:* African elephant, striding confidently through premises; Cutty Sark Hotel

🐘 *Middle right:* African elephant, eating trees on hotel property; Cutty Sark Hotel

🐘 *Lower left:* Legs of an African elephant and cattle egrets; Fothergill Island

Photograph next page:

🐘 *Feature:* Sunset, the day we learned Diana died; Hwange

157

Cutty Sark

Male and female created he them.

Genesis 1:27

Lake Kariba

Close Encounters

Almost every time
we saw lions, they came
close enough to touch.
Today, two walked
right by the Toyota.

No danger.
They both had their mind
on mating. Not even
tourists taking pictures
were going to stop them.

Just off Fothergill Island, we pull within five feet of an elephant knee deep, munching on reeds.

Lake Kariba
Boat Safari

Just off Fothergill Island, we pull within five feet of an elephant knee deep, munching on reeds.

A closer look at the eye of the elephant reveals nothing so expressive as the eye of a tiger,

except to say we examined his wrinkled lids and scraggly eyelashes and found there a lazy caution.

Lake Kariba

Camp title page:

Feature: Male and female lions, walking to mate; Fothergill Island

Premier camp photograph:

Feature: Tourists, encountering lions close; Fothergill Island

Photographs opposite page:

Upper right: Face of an African elephant; Lake Kariba

Middle right: African elephant's face, close-up; Lake Kariba

Lower center: Eye of an African elephant with scraggly eyelashes; Lake Kariba

Middle left: African elephant, munching on reeds; Lake Kariba

Photograph this page:

Feature: African elephant, knee deep, munching on reeds; Lake Kariba

Up a cozy inlet,
a herd of buffalo passes by,
the babies spaced strategically
between adult masses.

Lake Kariba

Photographs opposite page:

🐂 *Uppermost right:* African buffalo, Cape race, along shoreline; Lake Kariba

🐂 *Upper right:* African buffalo, Cape race, and tourists in Kariba Breezes motorboat; Lake Kariba

🐂 *Middle right:* African buffalo, Cape race, with cattle egrets and impala in background; Lake Kariba

🐂 *Middle left:* Motorboat; transport from Cutty Sark to Lake Kariba

🐂 *Upper middle left:* African buffalo, Cape race, and young, spaced between adults; Lake Kariba

🐂

Photograph this page:

🐂 *Feature:* African buffalo, Cape race, with red-billed oxpecker on back and cattle egrets; Lake Kariba

165

Tiny islands dot
the blue-studded waters,
havens for Egyptian geese,
spoonbills, storks, and herons.

A black-shouldered kite
glides overhead,
wings sweeping upward
and talons extended.

At sunset,
the buffalo graze;
a zebra, his skin rent
by lions, remains alert.

Lake Kariba

At a distance,
Fothergill Island is ablaze
with gas lanterns,
marking Batonka lodges

where we, entertained by a frog,
will shower under the stars
and sleep with a mosquito net
protecting our bed,

Photographs opposite page:

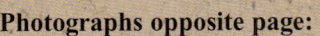 *Upper right:* Reed cormorants and gray-headed gulls
  in flight; Lake Kariba

Middle right: African buffalo, Cape race, at sunset;
  Lake Kariba

Middle left: Impala and plains zebra, Chapman's race,
  with skin rent; Lake Kariba

Upper center: Black-shouldered kite or osprey in flight;
  Lake Kariba

Uppermost left: African darter, landing on water;
  Lake Kariba

Photographs this page:

Upper right: Robert by Batonka lodge; Fothergill Island Lodge

Middle right: Swimming pool; Fothergill Island Lodge

Lower center: Frog on floor of bedroom; Fothergill Island Lodge

Lower left: Frog on edge of mosquito netting;
  Fothergill Island Lodge

Middle left: Marianne—photographer at work; Fothergill Island

Sanction

E gyptian geese,
     sacred birds of the Nile,
hunted to extinction there,
have made the rivers of Africa
their home.

We spotted two
along the Kariba shore,
lifelong mates,
so the guides say,
courting each other.

Shutting down
the motorboat engine,
we could hear
their evocative calls. She
with her high-pitched hur-hur,

and he with his guttural gasps,
circled each other,
stretching their necks
and flashing yellow
undertail coverts.

Lake Kariba

I don't know why
their image is carved
on ancient sarcophagi—
what mystery to kings,
what connection to the gods—

enigma inviolate.
I know only that
their beauty purifies them.
Like great lovers,
they will escape—

Cupid and Psyche
through an open casement,
Antony and Cleopatra,
surviving sin,
transcending consequence—

to the shadows,
the willowy and
hallowed images. . . .

Our boat drifting
close to shore
made them wary.
Brilliant blend
of chestnut and orange,

their orange eyes
marked us
before they took wing.

Photographs opposite page:

Upper right: Egyptian geese along shoreline; Lake Kariba

Middle right: Motorboat; transport from Lake Kariba to Cutty Sark

Lower left: Egyptian geese, marking photographer; Lake Kariba

Uppermost left: White-faced whisfling ducks in flight; Chobe

Photographs this page:

Uppermost right: White-faced whistling ducks in flight; Chobe

Upper right: Egyptian geese, one marking with his orange eye; Lake Kariba

Middle right: Egyptian geese, taking wing; Lake Kariba

Lower center: Egyptian goose, taking wing; Lake Kariba

Upper left: Cupid and Psyche by A. Santini; Burgoyne art collection

Playing at Life and Death

At Fothergill Island,
       our safari chanced upon
a lioness
and her two cubs,
only months old.
We watched them
frolic, lick each other's faces,
clean their own paws,
and yawn.
They are like watching
newborns;
every move they make—
for the record books.
Their mother, on guard,
made sure we didn't threaten.

The guides drove
up and down
the red dirt road,
trying to spy
a newborn family.
These littlest cubs
were nowhere.
Born in a lair,
blind,
helpless,
tucked away
in dens and crannies,
they are moved
every other day
by their mother.

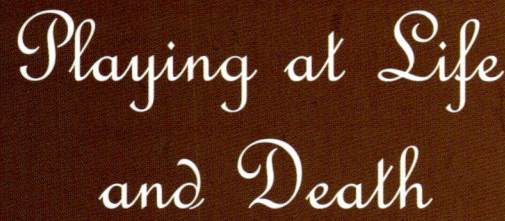

Lake Kariba

When we finally
glimpsed the babies,
they were deep in a thicket,
far from the road.
Although I zoomed them,
they were inaccessible.
No close-ups of
cute kitten faces
and teddy-bear ears.

The sad truth is
one of two will die:
an attack by hyenas
or an adult male
laying sexual claim
to the pride.
The saddest scenario:
abandonment
by their mother
should food be scarce.

The good news is
their mother is usually
their best ally.
She will defend them
even unto death
from males who
would kill them.
Still, she eats
until she is full
before she feeds them.

Photographs opposite page:

Upper right: Female lion, watching over cubs; Fothergill Island

Middle right: Lion cubs, looking at photographer; Fothergill Island

Far lower right: Lion cub, sneering; Fothergill Island

Lower center: Lion cub, yawning; Fothergill Island

Middle center: Lion cub, licking paw; Fothergill Island

Photographs this page:

Upper right: Lion cubs, deep in thicket; Savuti

Middle right: Female lion with cubs, drinking; Savuti

171

Back home,
I named the poor,
flame-colored stray
after these young lions.
"Isilwane" fits him;
he survived
his first three years
on his own,
as near as our veterinarian
can determine.

At some point,
he was abused,
kicked,
hit with a broom
or newspaper,
else this long later,
he would not still
be afraid of
my gentle husband—
runs from him
just because he fears
the man in his shoes
crossing briskly
over our wooden floors.

Lake Kariba

How much love
will it take to cure him?

I've seen him jump
on the back of
an attacking dog.

Isilwane is
my smart, wise,
mindful one,
my empathic soul,
my brave defender
of the property.

He loved Xaxaba.

He cried at my chest
when she first came to us.
He wanted me for himself.
Eleven months later,
he cried alone on the bed
when she went away
(to the veterinarian's)
and didn't come home.

Before we buried Xaxaba,
I showed him her corpse.
He sniffed her once,
assessed the loss,
and walked away.

Photographs opposite page:

🐾 *Upper right:* Isilwane in birdfeeder; Burgoyne backyard

🐾 *Far middle right:* Xaxaba, pining to jump up to birdfeeder; Burgoyne backyard

🐾 *Middle right:* Isilwane, licking and holding Xaxaba; Burgoyne bedroom

🐾 *Far lower right:* Isilwane on cement; Burgoyne front yard

🐾 *Lower left:* Isilwane, close-up; Burgoyne front yard

🐾

Photographs this page:

🐾 *Upper right:* Xaxaba, licking Isilwane; Burgoyne bedroom

🐘 *Middle right:* Marianne, coaxing Isilwane to bid farewell to Xaxaba; Burgoyne backyard

🐾 *Lower right:* Isilwane, licking Xaxaba; Burgoyne bedroom

🐾 *Lower center:* Isilwane, loving Xaxaba; Burgoyne bedroom

🐾 *Middle left:* Xaxaba, playing chase; Burgoyne backyard

🐾 *Uppermost left:* Isilwane on guard against Xaxaba; Burgoyne backyard

173

I know these cubs
will never be as safe
as my cats.
Why, if everything dies,
is it so sad
that in Africa most animals
die untimely?

I was melancholy—
no, more than that—
anguished,
found it unbearable
these babies could be
abandoned
until I watched
them stalk and ambush,
cuff each other,
take each other down,
like my Isilwane and Ihlosi,
"lion" and "cheetah,"
playing in my yard at home,
pouncing on each other,
mimicking a hunt.

And who's to say what fulfillment is?
Or how long it takes to achieve it?

Lake Kariba

Photographs opposite page:

🐾 *Upper right:* Lion cub, contemplating the universe; Fothergill Island

🐾 Far *middle right:* Lion cub, dozing; Fothergill Island·

🐾 *Middle right:* Isilwane, intimidating Ihlosi; Burgoyne backyard

🐾 *Far lower right:* Isilwane, dozing; Burgoyne backyard

🐾 *Lower center:* Ihlosi, annoying Isilwane; Burgoyne backyard

🐾 *Upper center:* Ihlosi, circling before attack; Burgoyne backyard

🐾 *Uppermost left:* Ihlosi, beginning attack; Burgoyne backyard

🐾

Photograph this page:

🐾 *Feature:* Lion cub—Here's looking at you; Fothergill Island

Photographs next page:

🐾 *Uppermost right:* Lilac-breasted roller, perched; Fothergill Island

🐾 *Upper right:* Blind; Fothergill Island

🐾 *Middle right:* African elephant, endowed, and cattle egrets; Fothergill Island

🐾 *Lower right:* Impala herd near edge of Lake Kariba; Fothergill Island

🐾 *Lower left:* African elephant and cattle egrets, walking; Fothergill Island

🐾 *Middle left:* Impala herd, minus one; Fothergill Island

🐾

*F*rom the blind,
   we see herds of impala;
      a bull elephant, endowed.

Lake Kariba

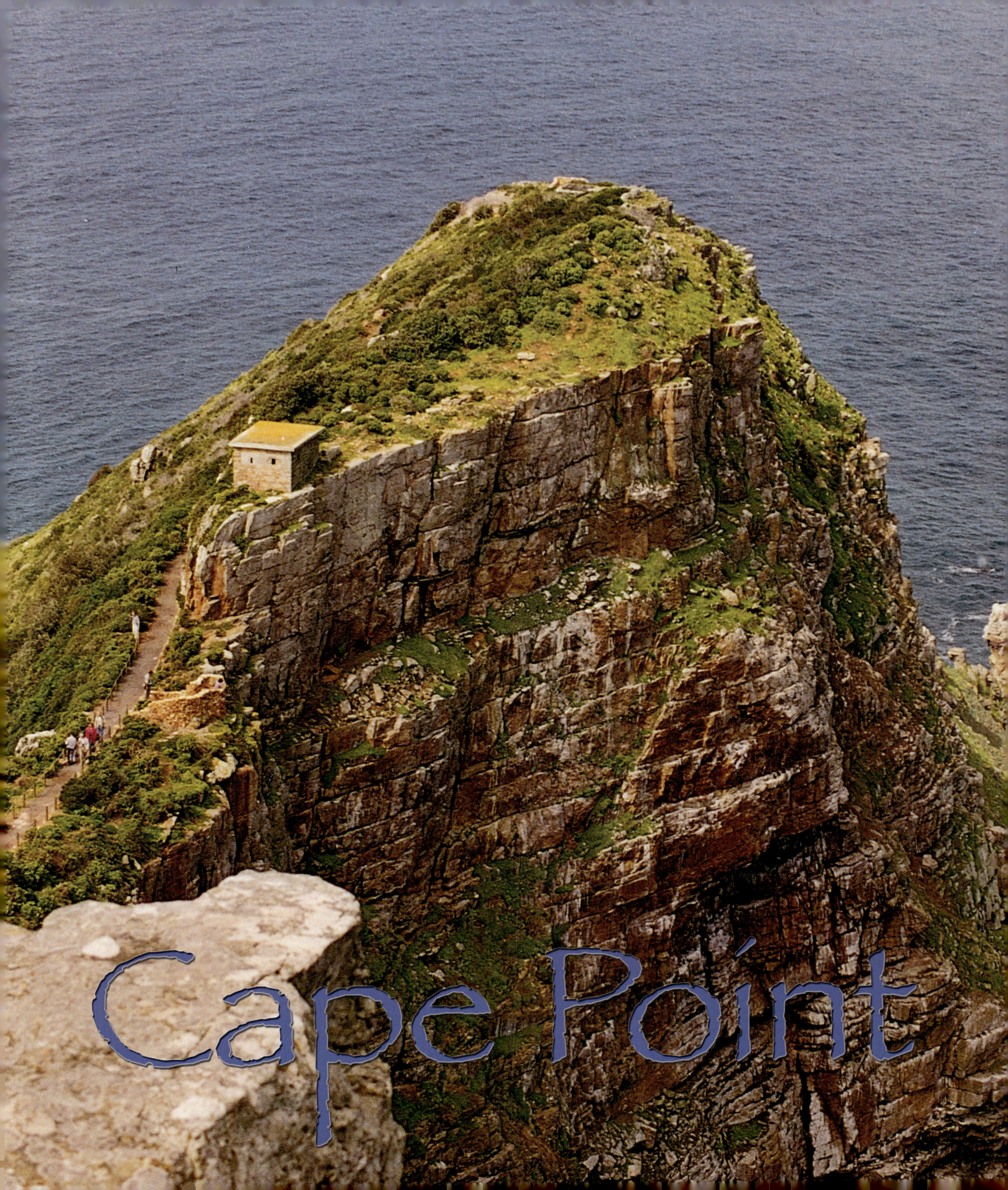

Cape Point

On our journey by private car from Cape Town to Cape Point,

...pped to photograph a bontebok, recently saved from extinction...,

The Dutch City

We arrived in Cape Town
the day of Diana's funeral.

Bustling harbor,
lights from the city dazzle at dusk—
jewels beneath Table Mountain—
sailboats dot a shimmering bay.

First settled by the Dutch,
supply base for their East India Company,
this is the city where Mandela
was imprisoned for eighteen years
at Robben Island
and then at Pollsmoor Prison,
from where he walked to freedom;
the city from where gold and diamonds
are exported, and good wine is made.

At Kirstenbosch Botanical Gardens,
birds of paradise and king protea,
wildflowers and fuchsias
bud along sweeping, sloping hills.

Nearing the end of our journey—
beauty everywhere—
an orange-breasted sunbird transforms
a pincushion protea;
sadness shadows and defines
our thousand selves—
like the telephone call
politely informing
our mother, our brother,
or our best friend is dead—
refining, redefining our
assailable souls.

Did Diana die with an unborn child?

So far from Ferron.
A tragic vision.
Unsafe,
at least today.

Cape Point

Camp title page:
🐾 *Feature:* Cape Point from land; southern end of Africa

Premier camp photograph:
🐾 *Feature:* Cape Point from helicopter; end of continent

Background photograph for Cape Point section, pages 180 through 196:
🐾 *Feature:* Cape Point from helicopter; end of continent

Photographs opposite page:
🐾 *Far upper right:* Wildflower; Kirstenbosch Botanical Gardens
🐾 *Upper right:* City by air and Table Mountain with tablecloth; Cape Town
🐾 *Middle right:* Sailboats in shimmering bay; Cape Town
🐾 *Lower right:* Sign; Pollsmoor Prison
🐾 *Far middle left:* Watsonias, "Arderne's White," blooming; Kirstenbosch Botanical Gardens
🐾 🐾 ●

Photographs this page:
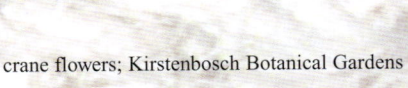
🐾 *Upper right:* Birds of paradise or crane flowers; Kirstenbosch Botanical Gardens
🐾 *Middle right:* Orange-breasted sunbird on pincushion protea; Kirstenbosch Botanical Gardens
🐾 *Lower left:* King protea at Huguenot home; Franschhoek
🐾 *Middle left:* King protea at Huguenot home; Franschhoek
🐾 *Upper left:* Bird of paradise or crane flower; Kirstenbosch Botanical Gardens

181

Extinction

On our journey by private car
from Cape Town to Cape Point,
we stopped to photograph
a bontebok, recently
saved from extinction,
now protected in the parks
of Cape Province.

"All these tests,
and no definitive answers,"
I heard the obstetrician say.
"But you will never conceive now."

The barren, empty womb
is heavy. I fret. No posterity.
I always ask, "What's going
to become of me?"
My DNA just stops.

Blesbok once thronged
the African highveld
in thousands.
Close to the cape,
small herds got separated,
then isolated,
when the Karooveld
formed millennia ago.
These animals,
confined to the coastal plain,
survived and evolved; hence,
their name change—
bontebok.

I heard him say it.
"You will never conceive now."

At my twenty-year reunion,
an old boyfriend said,
"Let me see your children;
I want to see what they look like."

The single male,
stately inheritor of the cape,

"She's my baby," I said to the veterinarian
that day from Kauai,
the last day of our vacation.
I was far away, helpless.
Xaxaba had been cut,
a deep wound slicing her back foot—
the babysitter couldn't say how—
the day of the Columbine shootings
in my birth state—Jen's twins
will go to high school there.

Now, three days later, the veterinarian felt
he should suture the wound,
a ten-minute surgery.
"Take safe care of her."
Again, I said it:
"She's my baby."

My husband fell on rocks,
the waves beating him down,
and again, and again.
People came from the beach
to help, pulling him to safety.
"High tide," I said.

I sat on the shore,
putting on my goggles.
The world turned dark,
too dark to see.
It was over—
I couldn't say what—
but it was over.
My husband had stumbled;
I had to go back.
"The waves—
they're treacherous," I said.
But he felt old; I could tell.

The red light was flashing.
"10:38 a.m. You have one message."
It was the veterinarian's voice
on the answering machine.
2:38 at home. He must have called

Cape Point

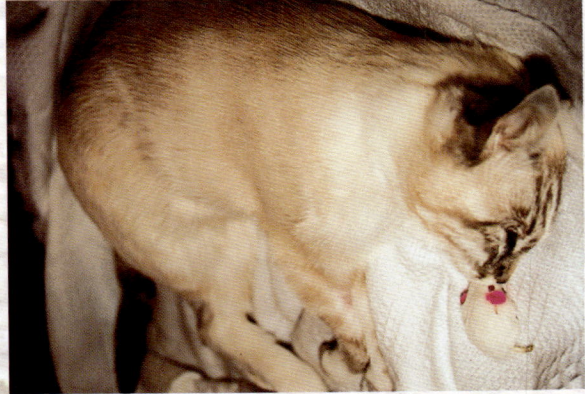

grazed behind a wired fence,
rather attractive
with his dark coat,
and wide, lightning blaze
flashing down his nose.

A generation later,
my niece did in vitro
and gave birth to twins.

"I would like to try
to get you pregnant,"
I heard him say.

Later, we glimpsed a small herd
from high on a mountaintop,
looking down to the coast,
where they roam protected,
nothing bigger than a jackal
to harass them.

In my heart, I believe
there are two sons.
I've named them:
Bradley Christian.
Justin Vincent.

a half hour after we left.
"There's been a real emergency
with Xaxaba."
I called him back.
Terror.

"Is she dead?" I asked.
"Yes."

It did matter what happened.
I tried to listen.
My heart was louder.
I stood in the shower and screamed,
shrill and then guttural.
"Oh, no"—I kept screaming it.
"Oh, God, no!
Not the baby."
For seven hours
on the plane ride home,
I said it:
"Not the baby.
Tell me it wasn't the baby."

But my husband knew
this was one thing
he couldn't fix.

And my daughter....
Strange.
I've never let myself
think of her until now.
My daughter—
I almost see her,
delicate—fragile—
and beautiful,
innocent as Eve,
so ethereal I haven't named her,
fine blonde hair streaming,
running barefoot through
the backyard myrtle,
running blissful,
running free.

Photographs opposite page:

Upper center: Bontebok in captivity; Cape Province

Far middle right: Bontebok in captivity; Cape Province

Photographs this page:

Upper center: Xaxaba's corpse; Burgoyne home

Lower right: Bontebok, grazing; Cape Province

Lower left: Bontebok, grazing; Cape Province

183

Off Guard

And then I saw her—
    an accident,
a vision,
a waking dream
waiting to happen—
the next spectacular child,
arms and legs flailing,
hurling through the air
from brother to brother,
landing halfway in between,
belly flop,
splash in the pool.

"Again," she yelled,
wiping hair from her face.
"Again."
Back to the first brother.
"Remember when we used her as a volleyball?"
"Hey, Missy," the second answered, "roll into a ball."
The child curled into fetal position.
Through the air, squealing.
Splash.
This time she went under.

And like a buoy,
up, yelling, "Again, again."
No one was enjoying this more than she.
Arms and legs out,
she'd squeal and hold her nose,
then flat, stomach first.
I thought it might hurt. Not so.

Cape Point

"Shouldn't we point her down
so she won't flop?" the first brother asked.
"Hold her high and angle her,"
the other suggested.
The girl was lifted to heaven and
aimed like a missile.
A torpedo now,
slicing the water.
"Again, again," she yelled.

I was the innocent bystander,
swimming laps at the Snowbird pool.
Her family was vacationing here.
I wasn't expecting to fall in love—
with a child—
and didn't realize
I was being wounded
until the third day.

That's when I asked one of her brothers
who she was.
He explained she had a special name
after a famous person, spelled differently,
"but we call her Missy."
"What's her last name?"
He told me twice,
but I was trying too hard to remember.
"How old is she?"
"Four and a half."
"Where are you all from?"
Again he told me,
and again I misheard it.

The next day,
studying at my computer,
I spoke with a friend, saying,
"I should be working,
but my heart is at Snowbird.
I want to see the child again."
My friend said, "Go then."

Photographs this, opposite, and next four pages:

All photographs on pages 184–189: Missy, siblings, and cousins at play; Snowbird

Missy is five and a half in all photographs except the two 4x6s on page 188.
There, she is seven and a half.

185

Her family had left that morning.
Someone at the pool said they left for home.

The last time I saw her,
she was standing by the side of the pool,
dressed in an American flag bikini,
her top red and white stripes, askew,
her bottom, white stars on a blue background.
She wanted to jump into someone's arms,
behaving like thousands of kids,
yet I never had seen anyone like her.

I came home and, days later, called 1411
for the little midwestern town I mispronounced.
At first, the operator didn't have
any surname close
to the one I hadn't quite got.
But then, she said, "Yes,"
and I knew those seven numbers
accessed a treasure.

I didn't call that day or the next or the next.
Instead, I cried for three months.

Cape Point

II

It took me more than a year to dial the number.
I may never have called,
but I got thinking
the resort was a time-share;
the family might return.
No one answered my first five tries.
All day.

Her brother remembered me.
He said she was coming to Snowbird in August.
I talked with her father.
He was polite.
I was polite.
I asked if she still had her flag suit.
"She has a new one this year,
but yes, it's downstairs in the bottom drawer."
I asked if I could photograph her "for the book."

I explained what had happened.
I had seen her.
I hadn't meant to fall in love.
Missy was the embodiment of a vision,
one I didn't think I would ever let myself see.
An innocent accident—
caught off guard.

I didn't say
she is like the sun
and the moon,
the dolphins,
the vanishing essence
of a dream.

187

Missy will never be my child.
She looks like her beautiful mother—
a gift to her, after she and her husband
lost her older sister.

I am richer for having known this child.
When I saw her again in August,
she wore her little flag suit, played
with her younger brother and cousins.
(Her two older brothers were working
with their dad back home—
no one to torpedo her.)

But she seemed more
like a mermaid,
mystical,
more beautiful than
I had remembered,
taller now, but still
a little girl.

After I took pictures,
she asked me questions:
"Why do you pin your hair up?"
"Will you take it down?"
"Do you live here?" meaning Snowbird.
"Do you have a house where I live?"
She was trying to make me fit.
"Do you have a kid?"
This was hard.
I answered, "I have kitties."
An innocent child.
She doesn't need me
to complicate her happy, happy life.
And I won't.

Cape Point

Mermaid

Unrequited, then.
When she gets older,
she may understand.
I understand.
I understand precisely all I have missed.

Not having a daughter like Missy—
Nothing that has happened to me—nothing—
not the cause,
nor the consequence—
has been sadder.
Not one thing.

Naming the Ephemeral

I am often my opposite.
Mercurial, so they tell me.
I see the vision.
Then I don't.
I know myself by names
not so sweet as
those by which I am known.

I fathom what it is to die—
and what to survive,
to rise like a scarlet ibis
in the midst of death,
to contemplate both sides
of a name, finding
an oxymoron in
every antithesis.

I spy a familiar stranger
in the Cape of Good Hope,
knowing Bartholomeu Dias
named it Cabo Tormentoso,
traveling through
so many storms.
John II renamed it
Cabo da Bôa Esperança
after Vasco da Gama
discovered a route
to the rich jewel of India.

Cape Point

Names are provisional.
The cape is both:
storms and hope.
I like to think
I can round the cape
and come out
undiminished,
reinventing who
I have always been:
the resilient woman,
suffering child.

After returning from
as far as Brazil,
Dias perished in a storm here.
But da Gama first fought his way
out of Calicut,
then returned to colonize,
forcing the raja
to make peace.
He sailed back to Portugal
via the twice-named cape,
triumphant, with a
rich cargo of spice.

Photographs opposite page:

 Upper right: Cape of Good Hope by helicopter; Cape Town to Cape Point

 Middle right: Robert and Marianne; Cape of Good Hope; photograph by driver

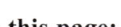 *Far lower right:* Blush beauties; Kirstenbosch Botanical Gardens

Photographs this page:

 Upper right: Cape of Good Hope from lighthouse; Cape Point

Middle right: Cape of Good Hope from lighthouse; Cape Point

 Lower left: King Protea at Huguenot home; Franschhoek

Helicopter Round the Cape

I asked John, our pilot,
"Is this flight safe?"
He answered,
"My last flight was."
I said, "Don't joke.
We nearly died,
taking off
from Amsterdam,
when the air baggage door
blew open over
the Atlantic Ocean."
But I could tell
I hadn't impressed him.

The rotors droned
so loud we resumed talking
by microphone.
Closer and closer to
Cape Point,
the wind blew
at a velocity of forty mph.
John said, "I have
to keep going up."
He looked at me,
"Don't worry,
if we went down,
you wouldn't hit the rocks
before you died;
the cold water
would kill you."

CAPE POINT
34° 21' 24" SOUTH LATITUDE
18° 29' 51" EAST LONGITUDE
SOUTH AFRICA

Cape Point

I stared at my husband.
It didn't matter
that we were wearing
life jackets.
Nothing would save us.
I thought for a moment
how insane we were,
courting ruin
just to see a shipwreck
rusting on a shore.

This illicit thrill pressed us,
and from the air,
we could see
why so many ships
sank, rounding the cape,
the ships clearing
the end of Africa,
then deceived by rocks
that jettison them
beneath the waves.

We journeyed
to the end of Africa
on a day the winds
were equivocal,
coming out
on the other side—
I'd like to say unscathed,
but not so—
not after so many years
of seeing too far into the sea,
so much suffering;
nevertheless, triumphant.
The vast Indian Ocean
stretched like a mosaic
made of lapis
to the east.

Photographs opposite page:

 Upper right: Helicopter 4344444; Cape Town

Middle right: Cape Point by air; Atlantic and Indian Oceans

Lower center: Robert, posing by sign; Cape Point

Middle center: John, our pilot; Cape Town

Photographs this page:

Upper right: Coastline; Cape Town to Cape Point

Middle right: Shipwreck along coast from helicopter; Cape Point

Uppermost left: Metal, rusting on shore from helicopter; Cape Point

193

Not only did we
get away with it,
we found whales
mating, thrashing
in the water below.
We circled low
to glimpse
their grandeur,
then pressed past
wine country,
flying between peaks
over cryptic lakes
atop Table Mountain.

Later,
our cab driver said,
"The helicopter pilots
are trained by the
South African army.
The government
can't take risks
with their million tourists."

The thrill,
the satisfying
hazard of it...,
and that is why
we spent the remainder
of our afternoon
making love.

Cape Point

Wine Country by Air: After a Vision of Cézanne

We are flying over
South Africa's wine country,
where I see lines and colors intersect
in a calculated geometry;
the fertile greens and browns
of fresh-tilled soil—
a patchwork of fields;
wineries scattered here and there,
displaced from one another.

They remind me
of a Colorado landscape—
farmhouses dotting green
and yellow alfalfa fields—
I saw time and again
as a child
driving with my father,
descending Rabbit Ears Pass
to Steamboat Springs,
when he, too masculine
to be aesthetic,
seemed awed each descent
by a vista so stunning;
and of Cézanne's painting
of his home in Aix-en-Provence:
house and aqueduct and roads
crisscross in dislocated strokes.

We circle high; shadows
of propeller blades
gyrate on whitecaps.
As with
Stein,
understanding
the fractured landscapes
of Picasso and Cézanne
only when she flew
above the land
in her first plane,
I see

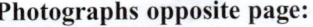

Photographs opposite page:

Upper right: A cryptic lake; Table Mountain

Middle right: Landmark, close-up, with tablecloth; Table Mountain

Far lower right: Blush beauties; Kirstenbosch Botanical Gardens

Photographs this page:

Upper right: Wine country by air; Cape Point to Cape Town

Middle right: Wine country by air; Cape Point to Cape Town

Far lower right: Wooden wine vat from Stellenbosch

Lower center: Wine vats WKD; wine country

Photographs next page:

Upper center and right: Whales, mating; Cape Point

Middle and lower right: King Protea; Huguenot home; Franschhoek

Lower center: Bird of paradise or crane flower; Kirstenbosch Botanical Gardens

Uppermost left: Whales' tails; Cape Town to Cape Point

hills rise in pyramids,
cut by the greens of trees
and the base of Table Mountain,
rising like Monte-Sainte-Victoire,
the largest mass of all,
simultaneously near and far,
as his shadow looms,

misplaced;
and then,

I am at boarding school,
studying modern paintings:
The woman was stripped,
auctioned,
men bidding for her uses.
Is it a woman
or a skeleton
screaming?
Could the lily
ever say no
to an intoxicating sun
and keep on living?
Why was that woman
tied naked,
draped over a barrel?

A landscape so serene: We lift—
Splendid!
Whales mate
between rotor slices
below.

Of my home,
and father—
good and wayward—
long forgotten.

Cape Point

It was our last day in the bush.

The perpetual cycle of Africa continues....

My final moments were spent

as if Africa meant to kiss me good-bye.

The Final Safari

It was our last day in the bush.
The perpetual cycle of Africa continues.
The impala herd huddled
in an open field; the lions circled
until they sent the impala scattering,
trapping one at the water's edge
where they ate their breakfast.

Later, I saw the lone mate
wandering back to the herd
and felt sad for those
beautiful creatures who survive
yet awhile longer. Sunrise
is not safe when lions are hungry.
Life is death in Africa.

My final moments were spent
as if Africa meant to kiss me good-bye.
We witnessed our final matings:
the preservation of life
and pleasant moments—
two young lions in love
or at least enjoying each other.

I hated to intrude, but this—
the lioness blissful and serene,
a queen content with male rivals
unable to contend with the partner
she had selected. And he,
as he rose up over her,
dominating; perfected.

Final Safari

Photographs opposite page:

Upper right: Fetching lioness on guard; Lake Kariba

Middle right: Female lion, rejecting unwanted male; Lake Kariba

Far lower right: Female lion and chosen partner, walking to mate; Lake Kariba

Lower center: Female lion—fetching feline; Lake Kariba

Middle center: Male lion—selected mate; Lake Kariba

Upper center: Impala—lone mate after kill; Lake Kariba

Photographs this page:

All photographs: Lions—mating sequence; Lake Kariba

Photograph next page:

Lower center: Marianne and Robert, home safe; Salt Lake International Airport; photograph by traveler

Camp title page:

Feature: Lions, mating; Lake Kariba

Premier epilogue photograph:

Feature: Male and female lions, relaxing; Lake Kariba

201

Primary Research Sources

Hosts, guides, and/or bushmen in individual safari camps.

Itinerary by African Travel.

On-site.

Maps.

Picture journal. Fifty-five rolls of film taken on twenty-three days of safaris.

Visitor's Center. Victoria Falls.

Secondary Research Sources

Alden, Peter C., Richard D. Estes, Duane Schlitter, and Bunny McBride. *National Audubon Society Field Guide to African Wildlife*. New York: Alfred A. Knopf, 1995.

Art Explosion: Clip Art. Calabasas: Nova Development Corporation, 2001.

Encarta Encyclopedia (1998). Microsoft Corporation.

Estes, Richard Despard, *The Behavior Guide to African Mammals*. Berkeley: University of California Press, 1991.

Johnson, Peter, and Anthony Bannister. Text by Creina Bond. *Okavango: Sea of Land, Land of Water*. New York: St. Martin's Press, 1984.

Lanting, Frans. *Okavango: Africa's Last Eden*. San Francisco: Chronicle Books, 1993.

Patterns in the Grass. National Geographic Video.